AL-QAEDA'S EXPANSION IN EGYPT: IMPLICATIONS FOR U.S. HOMELAND SECURITY

HEARING

BEFORE THE

SUBCOMMITTEE ON COUNTERTERRORISM AND INTELLIGENCE

OF THE

COMMITTEE ON HOMELAND SECURITY HOUSE OF REPRESENTATIVES

ONE HUNDRED THIRTEENTH CONGRESS

SECOND SESSION

FEBRUARY 11, 2014

Serial No. 113–52

Printed for the use of the Committee on Homeland Security

Available via the World Wide Web: http://www.gpo.gov/fdsys/

U.S. GOVERNMENT PRINTING OFFICE

88–169 PDF   WASHINGTON : 2014

For sale by the Superintendent of Documents, U.S. Government Printing Office
Internet: bookstore.gpo.gov Phone: toll free (866) 512–1800; DC area (202) 512–1800
Fax: (202) 512–2250   Mail: Stop SSOP, Washington, DC 20402–0001

COMMITTEE ON HOMELAND SECURITY

MICHAEL T. McCAUL, Texas, *Chairman*

LAMAR SMITH, Texas
PETER T. KING, New York
MIKE ROGERS, Alabama
PAUL C. BROUN, Georgia
CANDICE S. MILLER, Michigan, *Vice Chair*
PATRICK MEEHAN, Pennsylvania
JEFF DUNCAN, South Carolina
TOM MARINO, Pennsylvania
JASON CHAFFETZ, Utah
STEVEN M. PALAZZO, Mississippi
LOU BARLETTA, Pennsylvania
RICHARD HUDSON, North Carolina
STEVE DAINES, Montana
SUSAN W. BROOKS, Indiana
SCOTT PERRY, Pennsylvania
MARK SANFORD, South Carolina
VACANCY

BENNIE G. THOMPSON, Mississippi
LORETTA SANCHEZ, California
SHEILA JACKSON LEE, Texas
YVETTE D. CLARKE, New York
BRIAN HIGGINS, New York
CEDRIC L. RICHMOND, Louisiana
WILLIAM R. KEATING, Massachusetts
RON BARBER, Arizona
DONDALD M. PAYNE, JR., New Jersey
BETO O'ROURKE, Texas
TULSI GABBARD, Hawaii
FILEMON VELA, Texas
STEVEN A. HORSFORD, Nevada
ERIC SWALWELL, California

VACANCY, *Staff Director*
MICHAEL GEFFROY, *Deputy Staff Director / Chief Counsel*
MICHAEL S. TWINCHEK, *Chief Clerk*
I. LANIER AVANT, *Minority Staff Director*

———

SUBCOMMITTEE ON COUNTERTERRORISM AND INTELLIGENCE

PETER T. KING, New York, *Chairman*

PAUL C. BROUN, Georgia
PATRICK MEEHAN, Pennsylvania, *Vice Chair*
JASON CHAFFETZ, Utah
VACANCY
MICHAEL T. McCAUL, Texas *(ex officio)*

BRIAN HIGGINS, New York
LORETTA SANCHEZ, California
WILLIAM R. KEATING, Massachusetts
BENNIE G. THOMPSON, Mississippi *(ex officio)*

MANDY BOWERS, *Subcommittee Staff Director*
DENNIS TERRY, *Subcommittee Clerk*
HOPE GOINS, *Minority Staff Director*

CONTENTS

AL-QAEDA'S EXPANSION IN EGYPT: IMPLICATIONS FOR U.S. HOMELAND SECURITY

Tuesday, February 11, 2014

U.S. House of Representatives,
Committee on Homeland Security,
Subcommittee on Counterterrorism and Intelligence,
Washington, DC.

The subcommittee met, pursuant to call, at 3:15 p.m., in Room 311, Cannon House Office Building, Representative Peter T. King [Chairman of the subcommittee] presiding.

Present: Representatives King and Higgins.

Also Present: Representative Jackson Lee.

Mr. KING. Good afternoon. The Committee on Homeland Security, Subcommittee on Counterterrorism and Intelligence, will come to order.

Ranking Member Higgins will be here in a few moments. He has very kindly consented to allow us to start the hearing before he gets here, but he will be here just in a matter of moments.

The subcommittee is meeting today to hear testimony examining al-Qaeda's expansion in Egypt and the implications for U.S. homeland security, and I will now recognize myself for an opening statement.

Let me say at the outset, I really appreciate the witnesses coming in. I certainly regret the mix—the changes in the schedule today. Combination of the weather and trying to get enough people to vote on some key legislation involved the schedule for the day being changed around and, as usual, somebody else ends up being the victims.

You guys were the collateral damage, unintended victims here, but I appreciate your patience. Certainly—from going through your opening statements, I certainly appreciate the thoughtfulness you have given to this issue.

I will cut back on part of my opening statement other than to say that there is—there has been much speculation and thought that al-Qaeda somehow has been disseminated.

Many of us believe that, actually, the core al-Qaeda has been severely damaged. There are new franchises, there are affiliates, there are stand-alone organizations who share the same philosophy as al-Qaeda, and that really is the new threat that we face today.

We have seen that, obviously, in Yemen with al-Qaeda in the Arabian Peninsula. We have seen it in Iraq with al-Qaeda in Iraq. We have seen it with Boko Haram. We have seen it, to some extent, with al-Shabaab, who carried out the vicious attack in Kenya recently.

Even though we have had many counterterrorism successes in Afghanistan, diminishing the foothold and control of al-Qaeda there, even there, senior leaders are still present and waiting for the U.S. withdrawal of forces this year.

Of course, in our own country, we have many self-starters, we have self-radicalized and those who have been radicalized over the internet. But today's hearing is focused on the dangerous surge of terrorist activity in Egypt.

There has been significant reporting over the last few years about jihadist networks taking hold in the eastern Sinai Peninsula. These groups have launched attacks against the Egyptian military, against Israel, civilian shipping in the Suez Canal and other targets.

As is often the case with such safe havens, there are many gaps in our understanding of these groups. Their size, their relationship to one another, and their operational capability are not clear.

However, in the last month alone, terrorists have assassinated a senior Egyptian official, bombed the Cairo police headquarters, shot down a military helicopter, and fired rockets into Israel.

The speed with which these groups have gathered strength and conducted sophisticated operations not only in the Sinai, but in central Cairo, is noteworthy.

The apparent sophistication of these groups and indications that they are linked to al-Qaeda raise serious counterterrorism issues and emerging homeland security concerns. Egypt's role in the formation and history of al-Qaeda has made it a target for many years.

The Egyptian Ayman Zawahiri has led al-Qaeda since the death of bin Laden, and the ideology that inspired al-Qaeda was developed in Egypt by Zawahiri, who I said is an Egyptian.

His brother Muhammed was arrested outside of Cairo in August 2013 with speculation that he was working with jihadist networks in the Sinai.

Just last year, the Egyptian Muhammad Jamal Network was designated a foreign terrorist organization by the Department of State for its ties to al-Qaeda and for using the AQAP network to smuggle fighters into training camps.

However, what is perhaps most important is that these groups give strong indications of being allied and aligned with al-Qaeda's global jihad.

In his recent open testimony before the House Permanent Select Committee on Intelligence, when asked whether al-Qaeda affiliates in Syria presented a threat outside of Syria, the director of the CIA acknowledged "Any group that has its origins in al-Qaeda or are still associated with al-Qaeda presents a threat."

If this is true, working with the Egyptian Government to effectively fight jihadist networks in the Sinai should be a primary objective in our relationship with Cairo.

Unfortunately, the administration's decision to cut military aid in September has only hampered this effort and, I believe, displays a dangerous indifference to our shared interests with Egypt, which is defeating jihadist networks operating in the Sinai and throughout the country.

These groups threaten innocent Egyptians, American interests, and our ally Israel. Given what we have witnessed with the growth of AQAP, which prior to 2009, the United States did not consider posing a threat to the U.S. homeland, we have to monitor al-Qaeda elements in the Sinai for emerging threats to the homeland.

Furthermore, the instability caused by the Egyptian revolution has provided a period of time in which large groups of people moved into, out of, and around the country with less stringent oversight. Even so, removing a person's weapons and other illicit goods across Egypt's border with Libya and Sudan continues unabated.

For these and for other reasons, the potential exists that al-Qaeda-linked extremists could take advantage of a permissive operating environment to plan attacks against the United States.

This has heightened the need for the United States to work with the Egyptian and Israeli Governments on defeating and disrupting jihadist networks. Perhaps more than ever before, ensuring that Egypt can fight al-Qaeda is in the best interest of the United States.

As Chairman of the Subcommittee on Counterterrorism and Intelligence of this Homeland Security Committee, I feel it is necessary to begin a discussion on this emerging threat.

I look forward to hearing from our witnesses today and who these groups are, what they are capable of, and how to work with our partners to defeat them.

Now, with perfect timing, I am pleased to recognize for an opening statement the Ranking Member of the committee, Mr. Higgins of New York.

Mr. HIGGINS. With your permission, Mr. Chairman, I will suspend with my opening statement and submit it for the record. I know these gentleman have been waiting. So why don't we dive right into it.

[The statement of Mr. Higgins follows:]

STATEMENT OF RANKING MEMBER BRIAN HIGGINS

FEBRUARY 11, 2014

The United States relationship with Egypt is fractured and as we wait and see where Egypt's current political state leads the country, we must be mindful of our past relationship with Egypt while keeping an eye on any emerging threats from the region.

The United States has provided significant military and economic assistance to Egypt since the late 1970s. Between 1948 and 2011 the United States has given Egypt about $71.6 billion in bilateral military and economic aid.

Last month, this Congress voted to restore $1.5 billion in aid to Egypt. Aside from Israel, that is more money than the United States has given to any country. The United States has invested in Egypt to attempt to maintain regional stability.

In 2011, the Egyptian uprising caused the world to stop and watch as Egyptians revolted and caused the 30-year regime of Hosni Mubarak to end. In June 2012, there was hope for Egypt as it held a democratic election and elected Mohammed Morsi.

However, during his presidency, Morsi brought the nation to the brink of collapse and was not a legitimate ruler in the eyes of the majority of Egyptians. In July 2013, the Egyptian military removed its democratically-elected President Morsi and replaced him with its own regime.

Throughout the past months, there have been a series of deadly attacks in the region. Including a coordinated attack in Cairo last month. Additionally, freedom of the press remains stifled. Journalists have been detained.

The Egyptian economy is extremely unstable and the people do not feel safe in their own communities. One group that has emerged as one of Egypt's biggest threats is al-Qaeda-inspired Ansar Beyt al Maqdis (ABM).

ABM first emerged in 2011, amid a security vacuum caused by the fall of former President Hosani Mubrak. The group is based in the Sinai desert, next to the Israeli border. The group's operations expanded drastically after Mori was overthrown in July.

Egypt is a country in turmoil and our relationship with the country demands that there be some significant oversight given to the aid that we are providing.

This subcommittee also has the responsibility to examine what impact if any that ABM or any other terrorist organization operating in the Egypt has on the United States.

It is imperative that we examine these threats and their relevance, if any, to the United States interests in Egypt. It is also imperative that we hear from both the Government and private sector in open forum about Egypt and al-Qaeda's presence in that region and I hope future hearings will have Government witnesses.

Mr. KING. Thank you, Ranking Member. As I said, he is really a courteous, cooperative guy, before you got here.

Other Members of the committee, if they are not here today, are reminded that opening statements may be submitted for the record.

[The statement of Ranking Member Thompson follows:]

STATEMENT OF RANKING MEMBER BENNIE G. THOMPSON

FEBRUARY 11, 2014

For the past 3 years, the world has watched and witnessed change in Egypt. Since the Egyptian uprising, the country has been overcome with protest, unrest, and rapid political change. On February 10, 2011, after 18 days of fierce protests, former Egyptian president Hosni Murbak stepped down, ending a 30-year regime. In June 2012, Egypt had an historic election. The people elected Mohammed Morsi by a majority vote. In July 2013, the Egyptian military ousted Morsi.

In the months following the ousting of former President Morsi, the Obama administration suspended aid to Egypt while the State Department reviewed the military takeover and the new government's commitment to democracy during the transition. In addition to the United States cutting off funding to the government, there have been sophisticated attacks in Egypt. For example, in January 2014, coordinated attacks in Cairo killed 6 and injured 100.

According to the Egyptian government, Egyptian forces have arrested over a thousand terrorists since its transition from the Morsi regime. Violent attacks in a country that has been in turmoil and that has several extremist groups that call Egypt home should be of concern. What is also of concern is the recent crackdown by the Egyptian government on journalists and academics who have not been able to freely do their jobs in Egypt. The White House has asked the Egyptian government to drop the charges of the journalists and academics that are being held.

Last month, this Congress restored $1.5 billion in annual aid to Egypt. As an oversight body, this subcommittee is right in being concerned about the turmoil in Egypt and whether the fallout from this turmoil creates any direct threats to the United States or its interests abroad.

It is also a Constitutional mandate for this Congress to ask questions about the United States military and diplomatic actions in Egypt. However, this subcommittee's hearing strategy is ineffective. Like many of the hearings this committee and subcommittee have held this Congress, no one from the intelligence community has been invited to inform the Members about the threat and if there is imminent risk to the United States.

Nor is there anyone from the State Department here to testify and let the subcommittee know if the Egyptian government has successfully fulfilled the Congressional requirements to for the country to receive aid from the United States. While I look forward to the witness testimony today, I believe we are doing ourselves a disservice by not speaking with the appropriate administration officials in an open forum.

Mr. KING. We are pleased to have a distinguished panel of witnesses before us today on this important topic. Again, in the interest of time, I will limit my introduction of you, other—let me just emphasize and add how the Ranking Member and I are so privileged to have you—all of you here today and thank you for your contributions over the years.

We will begin with Dr. Steven Cook, who is a senior fellow for Middle Eastern studies of the Council on Foreign Relations.

Dr. Cook.

STATEMENT OF STEVEN A. COOK, SENIOR FELLOW, MIDDLE EASTERN STUDIES, COUNCIL ON FOREIGN RELATIONS

Mr. COOK. Thank you very much, Mr. Chairman. Thank you for the invitation to appear before you today to discuss the situation in Egypt.

For today's hearings, I will address what is happening in Egypt—oh, I am sorry. Rarely do I need a microphone. I am a New Yorker like you, sir—what is likely to happen in Egypt, the situation in the Sinai Peninsula, the potential effect on American interests, and what the United States can do about it.

A little more than 3 years ago today, I returned home after witnessing first-hand the exhilaration and hope of protesters in Tahrir Square.

Unfortunately, over the course of the last 36 months, Egypt's political development has not lived up to those aspirations. On the third anniversary of Hosni Mubarak's ignominious fall, political disappointment, enormous economic challenges, and an insurgency are Egypt's present and future reality.

The intention of those currently in power is to reengineer a political system in a way that makes it impossible for January 25, 2011, to happen again. The reconstituted political order is likely to be more brutal and more adept than its predecessors. Still, Egypt's leaders face obstacles to achieving those goals.

If there is one thing—one revolutionary thing that has happened in Egypt over the last 3 years, it is an emergence of large groups of people who are determined to continue to make demands on the Government through street politics and protests.

Second, based on experiences of the last 3 years, Egyptian politics can change very, very quickly. The political consensus around now Field Marshal Abdel-Fattah El-Sisi may be more apparent than real. That means that Egyptian politics are likely to be more contested going forward.

The authorities' only answers to this political ferment are authoritarian tools, notably, coercion and violence. This brings me to the situation in the Sinai Peninsula. The security problems there have become deeply, deeply worrisome.

It is important to note that it is the scale of violence that is new, not the problem of terrorism nor its cause. Egypt is, in many ways, a crucible of transnational jihad, as you noted in your opening remarks, and has produced a long list of notorious terrorists.

For at least a decade before the January 25 uprising, Israeli and American officials raised concerns to their Egyptian counterparts over the drug trade, the flow of weapons, human trafficking, and the presence of various extremist groups in the Sinai.

There is no evidence that President Mubarak took American Israeli concerns seriously. Even if he had, there are important political and structural impediments that would have prevented him from taking any—any effective action.

After the January 25 uprising, the Ministry of Interior was badly battered and the Ministry of Defense was consumed with running the country. This almost immediately resulted in the deterioration of security in Northern Sinai.

Attacks on police stations, bombings of the Trans-Arab and El Arish-Ashkelon pipelines, kidnapping of security personnel, efforts to infiltrate Israel, and brazen attacks on state facilities in the region's capital became frequent. This is a conflict that the Egyptian military is not well-equipped to fight.

Over the last 3 decades, with American help, Egypt's senior command had focused on developing a heavily-mechanized force complemented with air power. In addition, the officers have been resistant to American advice on how best to prepare for 21st Century threats.

Since the July 3, 2013, coup d'etat, there have been many, hundreds, of terrorist attacks in the Sinai and a series of attacks in major population centers in the Nile Valley, including Ismailiyya, Mansoura, the Sharqiya governate, and Cairo.

Ansar Bayt Al Maqdis is the primary al-Qaeda-affiliated group that has taken responsibility for those attacks, but other groups, including previously unknown—Ajnad Misr, Soldiers of Egypt, Jund al Islam, Soldiers of Islam—have also targeted the Egyptian state. Most ominously, in late July and again in early September, an extremist organization called al-Furqan fired on ships in the Suez Canal.

The Sinai is not yet an area of foreign jihadi activity. Like the low-level insurgency of the 1990s, however, the evidence suggests that violence in the Sinai is largely an Egyptian affair.

It may yet attract foreign jihadists, but thus far, the Sinai has enticed Egyptian nationals who have been fighting in Syria and Iraq to return home in order to wage war against what they believe to be an illegitimate government. Ayman Zawahiri, Egyptian leader of al-Qaeda, has offered his support to Ansar Bayt Al Maqdis and has encouraged Egyptians to take up arms against the state.

The best thing that the United States can do at this time is not cut aid from Egypt, but to support the Egyptians in this fight against al-Qaeda. The suspension of aid has not made Egypt more democratic and has not made Egypt less unstable.

The United States has a role to play in standing shoulder-to-shoulder with the Egyptians in this fight against terrorism going forward. Thank you.

[The prepared statement of Mr. Cook follows:]

PREPARED STATEMENT OF STEVEN A. COOK

FEBRUARY 14, 2014

Mr. Chairman and Members of the subcommittee: Thank you for this invitation to appear before you to discuss the situation in Egypt and how it affects U.S. National interests. For today's hearing, I will address broadly what is happening in Egypt, what is likely to happen in that country, the situation in the Sinai Peninsula, its potential to affect American National security interests, and what the United States can do to help the Egyptians meet the challenges they confront.

A little more than 3 years ago today, I returned home after witnessing first-hand the exhilaration and hope of protesters in Tahrir Square. Contrary to much of the commentary about that moment, economic grievances were not the primary factor that brought Egyptians into the streets. Rather, the crowd of tens of thousands that grew to hundreds of thousands 2 weeks later was demanding freedom, justice, dignity, and national empowerment.

Unfortunately, over the course of the last 36 months, Egypt's political development has not lived up to the aspirations of those heady 18 days in Tahrir Square. Instead, what we are seeing in Egypt is the reconstitution of a version of the old political order. The intention of those currently in power is to re-engineer the political system in a way that makes it harder for events like the January 25 uprising to happen again. This reconstituted order is likely to be both more brutal and more adept than its predecessor. Yet Egypt's leaders face significant obstacles to achieving their goal of stabilizing the political arena. The events of January–February 2011 do not constitute a revolution, but if there has been one revolutionary development in Egypt over the last 3 years, it is the emergence of large groups of people who are determined to continue making demands on the government through street politics and protest. Much attention has been paid to the Muslim Brotherhood in this regard, but opposition to the new order exists among the non-Muslim Brotherhood, non-religious end of the political spectrum. It is important to point out that although the January referendum on the new constitution earned overwhelming support, only 38.6 percent of eligible voters participated.

In addition, based on the experiences of the last 3 years, Egyptian politics can change very quickly. The Muslim Brotherhood's Freedom and Justice Party won a plurality of votes in the parliamentary elections in 2011–2012, but now many of its members are in jail or on the run. Egyptians applauded when Field Marshal Hussein Tantawi, the former head of the Supreme Council of the Armed Forces, ceded power to Mohammed Morsi after the June 2012 presidential elections, but a year later millions mobilized against Morsi, culminating in the coup d'etat of July 3, 2013. The political consensus since the military's intervention and the wide-spread popularity of Field Marshal Abdel Fattah al Sisi may be more apparent than real. This means that Egyptian politics will continue to be contested. The authorities' only answers to this political ferment are authoritarian tools—notably, coercion and violence. On the third anniversary of Hosni Mubarak's ignominious fall, political disappointment, enormous economic challenges, and an insurgency are Egypt's present and future reality.

This brings me to the situation in the Sinai Peninsula. The security problems there have become deeply worrisome. It is important to note that it is the scale of violence that is new, not the problem of terrorism nor its cause. Egypt is in many ways a crucible of transnational jihad and has produced a long list of notorious terrorists. For at least a decade before the January 2011 uprising, Israeli and American officials raised concerns to their Egyptian counterparts over the drug trade, the flow of weapons, human trafficking, and the presence of various extremist groups in the Sinai. There is no evidence that then-president Mubarak took American and Israeli disquiet seriously, but even if he had, there were important political and structural impediments that would have prevented him from taking any effective action.

First, the leadership in Cairo was not inclined politically to address to grievances of the population of northern Sinai, whether they be related to the lack of economic opportunity and development or to the poor treatment of the population at the hands of the Ministry of Interior. Although the Sinai is critical to a set of national myths related to past conflicts with Israel and national redemption, the area has not been incorporated into the political and economic life of the country. Given this neglect and the cultural differences between the largely Bedouin population of the Sinai and other parts of the country, residents of the Sinai do not feel Egyptian. To be fair, this situation is not necessarily unique to the Sinai. The same can be said of residents who live in the Nile Valley who also feel disconnected from the far-flung capital and its leaders who care little about developments outside the major population centers.

Second, Egyptian-Israeli security coordination was not as robust in the late 1990s and 2000s as it is now. During the mid-2000s, for example, there was considerable mistrust between the two security establishments in addition to thinly-veiled Egyptian anger over the efforts of Israel and its U.S.-based supporters to draw attention to Cairo's lackluster approach to the problem of underground smuggling from the Egyptian frontier to the Gaza Strip.

Third, and most importantly, the primary state organizations that were (and remain) responsible for the Sinai—the Ministry of Defense, the Ministry of Interior, and the General Intelligence Service (GIS)—have maintained different views on how to deal with problems there, have distinct missions, and are in competition with each other. Due to restrictions built into the Egypt-Israel peace treaty, the armed forces were only permitted in certain locations in the Sinai and only with certain pre-determined types of weapons. As a result, stability in the Sinai was largely left to the Ministry of Interior, which, as alluded to above, pursued its police functions with zeal and little regard for due process or human rights. For its part, the GIS was less interested in the quiescence of the population than it was in running intelligence operations in the Sinai. The inevitable result was the development of an environment conducive to crime, extremism, and violence.

After the uprising, the Ministry of Interior was badly battered and the Ministry of Defense was consumed with running the country. This almost immediately resulted in the deterioration of the security situation in northern Sinai. Attacks on police stations, bombings of the Trans-Arab and the al Arish-Ashkelon pipelines, kidnapping of security personnel, efforts to infiltrate Israel, and brazen attacks on state facilities in the region's capital al Arish all became frequent. Military operations during the summer of 2011 and 2012 did little to arrest this instability and violence. It is not accurate to suggest, as many in the media have, that the Sinai Peninsula is "lawless." There are informal legal institutions in the Sinai: Sharia courts are now taking the place of the tribal 'Urf court system, which the government under Mubarak was widely believed to have infiltrated. The spread of Sharia courts has become a way to propagate and institutionalize extremist ideologies and worldviews.

As the Egyptians celebrate today the third anniversary of Hosni Mubarak's fall, the insurgency that they are now confronting in the Sinai Peninsula is only one of many challenges, but perhaps the most serious one, that they face in the struggle to build a new and more just society. This is a conflict that the military is not well-equipped to fight. Over the last 3 decades, Egypt's senior command have focused on a heavily-mechanized force complemented by air power. The officers have also been resistant to American advice about how best to prepare for 21st Century threats. Since the July 3, 2013 coup d'etat, there have been at least 22 terrorist attacks in the Sinai and a series of attacks in major population centers in the Nile Valley, including Ismailiyya, Mansoura, the Sharqiya governorate, and Cairo. A group called Ansar Bayt at Maqdis (Supporters of Jerusalem) have taken responsibility for most of the attacks, but other groups including the previously-unknown Ajnad Misr (Soldiers of Egypt) and Jund al Islam (Soldiers of Islam) have also targeted the Egyptian state and security forces. Most ominously, in late July and again in early September, an extremist organization called al-Furqan Brigade fired on cargo ships in the Suez Canal with rocket-propelled grenades, though no damage was reported.

Observers have speculated that the Sinai Peninsula will or already has become a haven for foreign fighters intent on carrying out jihad. Like the low-level insurgency of the 1990s, however, the evidence suggests that the violence in the Sinai Peninsula is largely an Egyptian affair. The Sinai may yet attract foreign jihadis, but thus far the Sinai has enticed Egyptians nationals who had been fighting in Syria and Iraq to return home in order to wage war against what they believe to be an illegitimate government. Ayman Zawahiri, the Egyptian leader of al-Qaeda, has offered his support to Ansar Bayt al Maqdis and has encouraged Egyptians to take up arms against the state. There is currently a debate in Washington about Zawahiri and the extent of his control over al-Qaeda and its affiliates, but it seems clear that he maintain influence among Egyptian jihadists.

Mr. Chairman, this brief overview depicts a profoundly worrying situation of political uncertainty, economic deterioration, and extremist violence. This instability poses a threat to American National security interests including navigation of the Suez Canal, providing logistical support to U.S. forces in the Persian Gulf, overflight rights, and the preservation of Egypt-Israel peace. Since Hosni Mubarak's departure, the analytic community has been debating how the United States can best help Egypt. There have been many good ideas. Much of this work has, however, focused on promoting democratic development in Egypt. This is a laudable goal—one that I share—but Egypt's current trajectory suggests an unstable and authoritarian future.

In an environment where the Egyptian leadership and its supporters have characterized domestic politics as an existential struggle, there is little that the United States can do to help secure a democratic outcome. Washington should speak out forcefully and clearly against, for example, human rights violations, attacks on press freedoms, and policies that contradict the rule of law, but policymakers must understand that this is unlikely to have a decisive effect on the quality of Egyptian politics. Some observers have advocated suspending, delaying, or outright cutting U.S. military assistance to punish the military for the July 3 coup and to compel the officers to put Egypt on a democratic path. It is hard to understand how such a policy would advance democratic change or help improve Egypt's security situation. The Obama administration has already withheld important weapons systems from the Egyptians, including F–16s and Apache helicopters in response to the military's intervention, but this has not had a salutatory effect on Egyptian politics. Critics also argue that U.S. support for the military will further destabilize Egypt, reasoning that the officers' harsh crackdown is contributing to polarization and violence. This "repression-radicalization dynamic" is real, but whether the United States provides assistance or not, the military and the Ministry of Interior seem likely to continue to try to establish political control through coercion and violence. Withdrawing American support will not make Egypt less unstable.

Against the backdrop of this difficult debate, the United States has security interests in Egypt that virtually all observers agree remain important in the short run. The Egyptians have come to terms with the fact that they are likely to be battling extremists in the Sinai Peninsula for the foreseeable future. The Ministry of Defense is not always amenable to American advice because they fear that the United States wants to transform the military into a gendarmerie. There is no basis for this concern, but the Egyptians must break out of their outdated conception of security and rethink their doctrine to respond to the very real threats before them. This is where the United States can be most helpful, but to be successful, American policymakers will need to reassure Egyptian officers that Washington stands with them in the fight against terrorism and extremism. Specifically, the administration and the Congress should give the Egyptian military the tools and technology it needs to counter extremist violence; release suspended weapons systems, especially the Apache helicopters; establish a standing group of American and Egyptian officers to coordinate assistance coherently; and develop a trilateral American-Egyptian-Israeli security/intelligence/counter-terrorism mechanism that facilitates the flow of information among the security establishments of all three countries.

Mr. Chairman, my comments no doubt give rise to many questions and concerns and I look forward to discussing them with Members of the subcommittee. I am grateful to you for inviting me today and for holding this hearing on the difficult situation in Egypt.

Mr. KING. Thank you, Dr. Cook.

I should point out on the issue of—on the case of full transparency that Dr. Cook is a former constituent and his mother remains a constituent.

So I hope you report back to your mother and tell her I was okay.

Mr. COOK. I am hoping she will report back to you that I was okay, sir. Thank you.

Mr. KING. Thank you very much.

Our next witness is Tom Joscelyn, who has actually been a witness before this committee and subcommittee a number of times. He is a senior fellow with the Foundation for the Defense of Democracies and has been a strong fighter in the—and analyst in the war against terrorism.

Mr. Joscelyn, it is good to have you back again. Thank you.

STATEMENT OF THOMAS JOSCELYN, SENIOR FELLOW, FOUNDATION FOR THE DEFENSE OF DEMOCRACIES

Mr. JOSCELYN. Thank you, Congressman King and Congressman Higgins, for having me back again to testify before you about al-Qaeda and Egypt.

Now, real quick, the way I look at the threat in Egypt is that, after the revolution against Mubarak, what we witnessed were a number of al-Qaeda actors sort-of return to Egypt or got established in Egypt. This includes very senior al-Qaeda members who returned to Egypt or were released from prison.

Some of these al-Qaeda leaders actually returned from Iran, where they were harbored for years. Some of these leaders were actually referenced in Osama bin Laden's files as top al-Qaeda leaders that he wanted to protect and keep alive.

So that, I think, is a very underreported dynamic of what is going on in Egypt, that there are very senior al-Qaeda leaders who are, as far as I can tell, at large today.

I will just add this. We saw the threat of some of these senior al-Qaeda leaders actually on September 11, 2012. If you go back to the video footage of the assault on the U.S. embassy in Cairo, four—I have identified at least four very senior al-Qaeda jihadists who were involved in instigating those protests and shaping that event into a pro-al-Qaeda event, which led to the American flag being torn down and the al-Qaeda flag being raised over our embassy.

The second point that I would like to make is that what is happening in the Sinai right now is not necessarily confined to the Sinai, that it is actually part of an international network that is tied to other al-Qaeda actors both in Libya, Syria, and elsewhere. So it is not something that is just sort-of confined into what—in the Sinai Peninsula today.

We saw the threat that is emanating from the Sinai against U.S. interests already, I would argue, and one of the ways we saw that is that this group, Muhammad Jamal Network, which answered to Ayman Zawahiri, actually gauged some of the fighters to participate in the attack in Benghazi on September 11, 2012. There are— the Muhammad Jamal Network actually has camps in the Sinai— established camps in the Sinai, established camps in Eastern Libya and elsewhere.

Another threat that I think is underreported to American interests actually occurred last year, which is that the U.S. embassy in Cairo and other Western interests were actually—there was a plot to attack them by al-Qaeda terrorists, according to the Interior of Ministry in Egypt.

Again, the last time I testified before you gentlemen, we talked about al-Qaeda in Iran. What is interesting about this is that the same network that we talked about the last time I testified that gave us that plot to blow up a train from New York City to Canada was tied to this plot and to Egyptian actors that were targeting the U.S. embassy in Cairo.

So I think it is important to show the interconnectivity of all this and how the Sinai and these actors are not just sort of operating in isolation.

The third and final point involves what happens to the actors in the Sinai and Ansar Jerusalem, the main actor that has claimed responsibility for a lot of attacks.

Very carefully, if you go through the group's history, if you go through its operations, if you go through its statements, if you go through what senior al-Qaeda leaders have said about the group, it is, I would say, at a minimum, a pro-al-Qaeda or al-Qaeda-inspired type-of group.

I suspect that it is actually already operating as part of the al-Qaeda network. Why I say that is because, when you look at the specific operators involved, you look at the very granular details, you find all this connectivity to al-Qaeda's international network.

In September of last year, a suicide bomber, a former major in the Egyptian Army, blew himself up trying to attack a top Egyptian official and, when you go through his biography and the details of what we know about him or what the Egyptians say about him, I count at least five or six major points of connectivity to the al-Qaeda international network. This shows you that this group is actually operating as part of what al-Qaeda wants, basically, in Egypt.

When you go through Ayman Zawahiri and senior al-Qaeda leaders' statements about the group, it is pretty eerie to see that they continually approve of the group's operations, they continuously single out bombings on pipelines, rocket attacks, any—what have you, to say that this is basically what they want and what Muslims should be doing in Egypt, what jihad should be doing in Egypt, to carry the fight forward.

So when you look at it from that perspective, I think that, as the story of Ansar Jerusalem has evolved over time, its ties to al-Qaeda's international network are getting stronger. The evidence is those ties are getting stronger, not weaker. Okay?

So this isn't necessarily—it could be just an al-Qaeda-inspired group that was an upstart that is trying to gain the—basically, support of the al-Qaeda network. I think that it may be something other than that. I think it may be sort-of a group that has basically been implanted by al-Qaeda actors to grow and operate.

On that last point, I will say this, too. Congressman King, you mentioned al-Qaeda in the Arabian Peninsula. As you can see in my written testimony, I think there is strong evidence that al-Qaeda in the Arabian Peninsula is actually operating in the Sinai, that, in fact, they have ties to terrorists in the Sinai. I gave you a number of reports in my written testimony along those lines.

That is obviously important for the reasons you pointed out, which this is a group that has sort-of carried the banner of the fight against the United States and has launched numerous attacks against the United States. This may be something that they see the Sinai as a crossroads for sort-of further operations in the future.

Thank you.

[The prepared statement of Mr. Joscelyn follows:]

PREPARED STATEMENT OF THOMAS JOSCELYN

FEBRUARY 11, 2014

Chairman King, Ranking Member Higgins, Members of the committee, thank you for inviting me here today to discuss al-Qaeda's presence in Egypt. The uprisings throughout the Muslim world that began in late 2010 and early 2011 brought hope to millions of people. Al-Qaeda did not instigate these revolts, but in the years since the group has exploited the security vacuums created in their wake.

Al-Qaeda's theory of the revolution in Egypt, and the subsequent overthrow of Mohamed Morsi's Islamist regime, is predicated on its deeply anti-American and anti-Semitic worldview. Al-Qaeda's senior leaders portrayed Mubarak's fall as a defeat for the United States and its interests in the region. For instance, al-Qaeda head Ayman Zawahiri portrayed the toppling of dictators in Egypt and Tunisia as comparable to America's military losses and the September 11, 2001, terrorist attacks. America "was defeated in Tunisia and lost its agent there," Zawahiri said in an October 2011 recording, and "it was defeated in Egypt and lost its biggest agent there."[1]

Even though al-Qaeda has long disagreed with the Muslim Brotherhood's approach to politics, sometimes vehemently so, the group did not call for jihad against

---

[1] SITE Intelligence Group, "Zawahiri Praises Libyan Rebels, Eilat Attackers; Urges Algerians to Revolt," October 11, 2011.

Morsi or his government. Instead, most of post-Mubarak Egypt became a land for proselytization. In "Egypt and Tunisia, the opportunities have opened up for preaching [but] only Allah knows how long they will last," Zawahiri said in an August 2011 message. "Therefore," Zawahiri continued, "the people of Islam and jihad should benefit from them and take advantage of them to report the clear truth and make the Ummah come together around the primary issues that no Muslim can dispute."[2] Accordingly, from early 2011 through the middle of 2013, Zawahiri's henchmen and allied jihadists set up organizations to spread al-Qaeda's ideology. They preached in Tahrir Square, appeared on national television, and openly operated in a country where they had once been hunted and harassed by security services.

In some respects, however, the Sinai was different. The jihadists saw it as a new front for confronting Israel and a base for their operations. Various al-Qaeda-linked or inspired groups grew. When Egyptian security forces conducted counterterrorism raids, they became viable terrorist targets. Indeed, al-Qaeda's leaders repeatedly condemned Egypt's military even prior to Morsi's ouster. When Morsi was deposed in early July 2013, the landscape changed once again. No longer was the Islamist regime, which al-Qaeda saw as doomed to fail, in power. Al-Qaeda has consistently portrayed the Egyptian military as a servant of an imaginary Zionist-Crusader conspiracy, making the government a legitimate target for jihad.

Egypt continues to pose of a variety of counter-terrorism challenges and threats to American interests. I address several of these areas of concern in my testimony today.

- *Al-Qaeda likely has "core" leaders inside Egypt today.*—During and after the 2011 uprisings, senior jihadists allied with al-Qaeda were freed. Others returned from abroad, including from Iran, which offered Egyptian jihadist leaders a form of safe haven for years. Not all of these jihadists returned to terrorism, but some influential jihadists did. The September 11, 2012, protest in front of the U.S. Embassy in Cairo, which turned into an all-out assault, was instigated by "old school" jihadists who are part of al-Qaeda's network and were freed after Mubarak's fall.

  After President Mohamed Morsi's regime was overthrown, the military and security forces re-arrested a number of senior jihadist figures. However, some likely remain active and may hold leadership roles in new al-Qaeda-allied terrorist organizations.

- *The Muhammad Jamal Network (MJN), which was established in 2011, is an international threat and part of al-Qaeda's network.*—One of the "old school" Egyptian Islamic Jihad (EIJ) jihadists released from prison in 2011 is Muhammad Jamal, a long-time subordinate to Ayman Zawahiri. Despite Jamal's re-imprisonment in late 2012, the MJN remains active today in the Sinai, mainland Egypt and elsewhere. The MJN clearly operates as part of al-Qaeda's international network and has ties to terrorists in Europe. Some of its members participated in the September 11, 2012, terrorist attack in Benghazi, Libya. Egyptian authorities have alleged that the MJN was connected to an al-Qaeda plot against Western embassies and other interests in Cairo in 2013.[3]

- *There is strong evidence indicating that al-Qaeda in the Arabian Peninsula (AQAP), which is headquartered in Yemen, is operating in the Sinai.*—This is an important development because AQAP has repeatedly attempted to attack the U.S. homeland since 2009 and is increasingly managing al-Qaeda's assets far from its home base of operations. The head of AQAP, Nasir al Wuhayshi, is the general manager of al-Qaeda's global network.

- *The Sinai Peninsula has become home to multiple al-Qaeda actors, as well as al-Qaeda-inspired groups.*—Osama bin Laden's former doctor is reportedly a senior al-Qaeda leader in the Sinai today. Several groups proclaiming their allegiance to al-Qaeda have emerged in the Sinai since 2011.

- *Ansar Jerusalem (Ansar Bayt al-Maqdis), the most prolific Sinai-based jihadist organization, is pursuing al-Qaeda's agenda.*—Al-Qaeda's leader, Ayman Zawahiri, has repeatedly praised the group's attacks. Ansar Jerusalem shares al-Qaeda's ideology, employs al-Qaeda's tactics, and routinely refers to and praises al-Qaeda's leaders in its statements. There is much we do not know about Ansar Jerusalem's operations, but a growing body of evidence suggests it is tied to al-Qaeda's international network.

---

[2] SITE Intelligence Group, "Zawahiri Rallies for Jihad; Calls for Intellectual Debate, Advocacy," August 15, 2011.

[3] Thomas Joscelyn, "Egyptian interior minister: Al Qaeda cell plotted suicide attack against Western embassy," *The Long War Journal*, May 11, 2013. (*http://www.longwarjournal.org/archives/2013/05/egyptian_interior_mi.php*)

- *The Muslim Brotherhood, or at least elements of the organization, may have already turned to violence.*—The overthrow of Mohamed Morsi's regime was an "I told you so" moment for al-Qaeda. The organization's senior ideologues have long argued that an Islamist regime would not be allowed to rule Egypt. Brotherhood members are certainly disillusioned following Morsi's ouster, and al-Qaeda may, therefore, be more appealing to them. We know that groups such as Ansar Jerusalem are already poaching from the Brotherhood's ranks. Egyptian officials have leveled a number of allegations against the Brotherhood, saying that it is deeply involved in supporting terrorist activities. These allegations may be false and designed to further delegitimize the Brotherhood at home and abroad. However, some of the allegations are specific and can, therefore, be either verified or rejected. During the Brotherhood's brief reign, Morsi and others did cooperate with jihadists in some ways. This entire subject is murky and requires more analysis.
- *Finally, it is worth stressing that al-Qaeda views the Sinai as a base of operations for fighting an imaginary "Zionist-Crusader" conspiracy.*—That is, al-Qaeda sees the Sinai as a launching pad for attacks against both American and Israeli interests. Today, Israel faces more of a challenge from jihadists allied with al-Qaeda than ever before. This threat comes not just from the Sinai, but also from other countries, including Syria.

Below, I have divided the rest of my written testimony into three sections. In the first section, I outline how key al-Qaeda leaders (including "core" members) became active in Egypt following the revolution. Some of them are still active to this day. In the second section, I give a brief overview of the leading al-Qaeda-linked organizations in the Sinai. In the third and final section, I look at Ansar Jerusalem more closely, demonstrating that the organization is clearly pursuing al-Qaeda's agenda.

POST-REVOLUTION: AL-QAEDA LEADERS BECOME ACTIVE IN EGYPT

For decades, the main terrorist challenge to the Egyptian government came from the Egyptian Islamic Jihad (EIJ) and Gamaa Islamiyya (IG), two groups that were allied with al-Qaeda and responsible for high-profile attacks on both Egyptian leaders and civilians. The EIJ was headed by Ayman Zawahiri and merged with Osama bin Laden's venture prior to the September 11, 2001, terrorist attacks. While some IG leaders renounced violence from behind bars in Egypt, others did not and remained loyal to al-Qaeda. Long-time IG spiritual leader Sheikh Omar Abdel Rahman, a.k.a. "the Blind Sheikh," remains a popular figure in jihadist circles 2 decades after his imprisonment in the United States.

Under Hosni Mubarak's regime, many EIJ and IG leaders were imprisoned. Some avoided confinement by staying abroad, either in Afghanistan-Pakistan, Iran, or elsewhere. After Mubarak's fall, dozens of EIJ and IG leaders were freed from prison. Still others returned to their home country, where they were suddenly acquitted of long-standing terrorism charges.

One such key al-Qaeda leader is Mohammad Islambouli, the brother of Anwar Sadat's assassin. Islambouli lived in Iran for years after 9/11. While living in Iran, he was a part of an IG contingent that formally merged with al-Qaeda. In fact, Islambouli's ties to al-Qaeda leadership go back decades. His importance can be seen in the limited number of documents released from Osama bin Laden's compound in Abbottabad, Pakistan. In one document, dated October 20, 2010, bin Laden stresses the importance of protecting Islambouli, who had apparently evacuated northern Pakistan (after leaving Iran) for Kunar, Afghanistan. "He should be informed of the nature of work and he should be consulted on things that are being discussed," bin Laden writes, in reference to some on-going projects.[4] An earlier document, dated March 28, 2007, is addressed to an individual known as "Adnan Hafiz Sultan," who is also referred to as the "maternal uncle."[5] The latter phrase ("maternal uncle") is al-Qaeda's coded reference for Islambouli.[6] If this letter is addressed to Islambouli, and it certainly appears that it is, then its contents show how Islambouli is a part of al-Qaeda's senior leadership and he has been involved in managing the group's operations in Iraq and elsewhere.

After returning to Egypt, Islambouli was reportedly freed by an Egyptian military court in 2012 despite having been convicted of terrorism charges in absentia decades

---

[4] SOCOM–2012–0000015. Islambouli is referred to as Muhammad Shawqi Abu-Ja'far in the document.

[5] SOCOM–2012–0000011.

[6] Bill Roggio, Daveed Gartenstein-Ross, and Tony Badran, "Intercepted Letters from al-Qaeda Leaders Shed Light on State of Network in Iraq," *The Long War Journal*, September 12, 2008. *(http://www.defenddemocracy.org/media-hit/intercepted-letters-from-al-qaeda-leaders-shed-light-on-state-of-network-in/).*

14

earlier.[7] It is not clear where Islambouli is today, or if he has been re-arrested. But Islambouli's re-emergence demonstrates how an Egyptian al-Qaeda leader, important enough for bin Laden to protect, suddenly found his home country to be hospitable once again. And Islambouli was not the only IG member turned senior al-Qaeda leader to return from abroad in 2011 and 2012.

In addition, a contingent of EIJ leaders loyal to al-Qaeda's leader became especially active inside Egypt after their release from prison. They were led by Mohammed Zawahiri, the younger brother of Ayman Zawahiri. Until he was re-arrested in 2013, Mohammed Zawahiri used the permissive environment following the fall of Mubarak to proselytize, often under the banner of "Ansar al Sharia Egypt." This group was established by one of his former EIJ comrades, Ahmed Ashush. In interviews, Ashush proclaimed his allegiance to al-Qaeda, saying that he was "honored to be an extension of al-Qaeda."[8] Although Mohammed Zawahiri spent much of his trying to win new converts for al-Qaeda's ideology, he likely returned to terrorist operations and was in contact with his brother as well.[9]

Mohammed Zawahiri was one of the chief instigators of the September 11, 2012, protest in front of the U.S. Embassy in Cairo. The protest turned into an all-out assault on the compound, with the stars and stripes being ripped down and replaced by al-Qaeda'a black banner. The protest-turned-assault was a pro-al-Qaeda event from the first, with protesters openly praising Osama bin Laden and al-Qaeda. I have identified at least three other senior al-Qaeda-linked jihadists who helped spark the protest: Tawfiq Al 'Afani, 'Adel Shehato, and Rifai Ahmed Taha Musa.[10] Al 'Afani and Shehato are long-time EIJ ideologues and leaders. Shehato has since been re-arrested and charged with leading the so-called Nasr City Cell, which had multiple ties to al-Qaeda.[11]

Rifai Ahmed Taha Musa once led the IG and was a close confidante of the Blind Sheikh. He was very close to Osama bin Laden and Ayman Zawahiri. He even signed al-Qaeda's 1998 fatwa declaring the formation of a "World Islamic Front for Confronting the Jews and Crusaders."[12] The CIA considered Taha Musa to be such an important terrorist that he was tracked down in Syria, where he was detained and deported to Egypt in late 2001.[13]

Dozens of other senior al-Qaeda-linked jihadists either returned to Egypt or were freed from prison following the revolution. This raises several concerns going forward.

First, these jihadists were able to build up their operations with only occasional interference from security forces for approximately 2 years. They likely established terrorist cells and played a role in establishing some of the groups now based in the Sinai.

Second, while some of these leaders have been re-imprisoned, there are unconfirmed reports that top jihadists such as Mohammed Zawahiri and Muhammad Jamal continue to communicate with the outside world from prison. Others remain free.

Third, al-Qaeda's senior leadership is filled with Egyptians (including Saif al Adel, an al-Qaeda leader still wanted for his role in the 1998 U.S. Embassy bombings), who know their home country well and have thick roots in the jihadist scene there.

---

[7] "Egypt military court releases the brother of Sadat's assassin," *Ahram Online,* February 27, 2012. *(http://english.ahram.org.eg/NewsContent/1/64/35491/Egypt/Politics-/Egypt-military-court-releases-the-brother-of-Sadat.aspx).*

[8] Thomas Joscelyn, "Ansar al Sharia Egypt founder 'honored to be an extension of al Qaeda'," *The Long War Journal,* November 27, 2012. *(http://www.longwarjournal.org/archives/2012/11/ansar_al_sharia_egyp.php)* For additional articles concerning Ansar al Sharia Egypt's ties to al-Qaeda-linked terrorists see: *http://www.longwarjournal.org/tags/Ansar%20al%-20Sharia%20Egypt/common/.*

[9] For example, see: Siobhan Gorman and Matt Bradley, "Militant Link to Libya Attack," *The Wall Street Journal,* October 1, 2012. *(http://online.wsj.com/news/articles/SB10000872396390444549204578020373444418316)* Some of Zawahiri's recruits went on to carry out suicide operations. See: Thomas Joscelyn, "Follower of Mohammed al Zawahiri dies in attack in Mali," *The Long War Journal,* May 10, 2013. *(http://www.longwarjournal.org/archives/2013/05/follower_of_mohammed.php)*

[10] Thomas Joscelyn, "Al Qaeda-linked jihadists helped incite 9/11 Cairo protest," *The Long War Journal,* October 26, 2012. *(http://www.longwarjournal.org/archives/2012/10/al_qaeda-linked_jiha.php)*

[11] See: Thomas Joscelyn, "Egypt arrests pro-al Qaeda jihadist tied to Benghazi suspect," *The Long War Journal,* November 2, 2012. *(http://www.longwarjournal.org/archives/2012/11/egyptian_islamic_jih.php)* and Thomas Joscelyn, "More al-Qaeda links to Cairo terror cell reportedly found," *The Long War Journal,* November 9, 2012.

[12] Taha Musa would later claim that his name was mistakenly included on the fatwa.

[13] For an overview of Taha Musa's al-Qaeda role, see: Thomas Joscelyn, "Al Qaeda-Linked Jihadists Incited Cairo Protest," *The Weekly Standard,* October 26, 2012. *(http://www.weeklystandard.com/blogs/al-qaeda-linked-jihadists-incited-cairo-protest_657859.html)*

This gives al-Qaeda's leaders a clear opportunity to leverage their historical ties with any jihadists who remain free.

The Sinai has long been plagued by terrorism, among its many other problems. But since the ouster of Mohamed Morsi there has been a stunning increase in the violence. As my colleague at the Foundation for the Defense of Democracies David Barnett has documented, there have been more than 300 reported attacks in the Sinai from July 3, 2013 through February 6, 2014. This violence has spilled over into the mainland, as Sinai-based groups are increasingly executing high-profile attacks in Egypt's densely-populated urban areas.

There are credible reports of contacts between terrorists in the Sinai and al-Qaeda's senior leadership. In late July 2013, Ayman Zawahiri joined a "conference call" of more 20 al-Qaeda operatives around the globe that included "aspiring al-Qaeda affiliates operating in the Sinai."[14] Zawahiri's contact with the Sinai jihadists reportedly prompted the closing of the U.S. Embassy in Tel Aviv. Other U.S. diplomatic facilities around the globe were closed because of the possibility of an impending terrorist attack. There are unconfirmed reports of handwritten communications from Zawahiri to terrorists in the Sinai.[15] Egyptian security officials have alleged that the interrogations of terrorist suspects have revealed ties between the Sinai jihadists and "groups which operate in Afghanistan and Pakistan, as well as other countries not just Gaza."[16] As I discuss more below, Muhammad Jamal, who established training camps in the Sinai, was in direct contact with Zawahiri.

Several al-Qaeda-inspired and/or al-Qaeda-linked groups operate in the Sinai today. These include Ansar Bayt al-Maqdis (Ansar Jerusalem), al-Qaeda in the Sinai Peninsula (AQSP) and Ansar al Jihad, the Muhammad Jamal Network (MJN), the Mujahideen Shura Council in the Environs of Jerusalem (MSC), Al Salafiya Al Jihadiya in Sinai (Salafi Jihadist Movement in the Sinai), and al Tawhid wal Jihad, among others. In addition, al-Qaeda in the Arabian Peninsula (AQAP) has established a presence in the Sinai. Untangling this web of groups is extremely difficult, if not impossible. There is collusion between at least some of these groups. And it is possible that some of these organizations overlap, sharing a common infrastructure while operating under different names.

In this section, I provide a brief overview of four of these organizations, before moving on to a longer treatment of Ansar Jerusalem. These five organizations are the most operationally relevant.

Al-Qaeda in the Sinai Peninsula (AQSP) and Ansar al Jihad

In late July 2011, masked gunmen attacked a police headquarters in Arish and a gas pipeline. By some accounts, approximately 100 terrorists were involved in the attack. During the initial arrests, 10 Palestinians were identified as being among the attackers.[17] Shortly after the assault, a statement was issued by a group calling itself al-Qaeda in the Sinai Peninsula (AQSP). The statement called for the creation of an Islamic emirate in the Sinai. AQSP also called on the Egyptian Army to disregard the Camp David Accords and to end the "siege" in Gaza.[18]

The reported emir of AQSP, which has been blamed for a string of attacks, is Ramzi Mowafi, Osama bin Laden's former physician.[19] Mowafi is believed to be an explosives expert and to have worked on chemical weapons for al-Qaeda. Mowafi is another example of the phenomenon of "old school" jihadists returning to the fight.

Another group calling itself Ansar al Jihad in the Sinai Peninsula is believed to be the military wing of AQSP. Ansar al Jihad announced its formation in December 2011, saying it vowed to "fulfill the oath" of slain al-Qaeda leader Osama bin

---

[14] Eli Lake and Josh Rogin, "Exclusive: U.S. Intercepted Al Qaeda's 'Legion of Doom' Conference Call," *The Daily Beast,* August 7, 2013. *(http://www.thedailybeast.com/articles/2013/08/07/al-qaeda-conference-call-intercepted-by-u-s-officials-sparked-alerts.html)* The "conference call" actually utilized a sophisticated internet-based communications system.

[15] "Egypt's North Sinai Security Chief: We Are Chasing Ghosts in the Sinai," *Al-Dustur Online* (Cairo), November 11, 2012.

[16] *Al-Misri al-Yawm,* August 1, 2013.

[17] Jailan Halawi, "Egypt: Al-Qaeda in Sinai?," *Al-Ahram Weekly,* August 4, 2011.

[18] "Security operation continues in North Sinai," *Daily News Egypt,* August 17, 2011.

[19] David Barnett, "Former bin Laden doctor reportedly heads al Qaeda in the Sinai Peninsula," *The Long War Journal,* July 17, 2013. *(http://www.longwarjournal.org/archives/2013/07/former_bin_laden_doc.php).*

Laden.[20] Ansar al Jihad swore allegiance to al-Qaeda emir Ayman Zawahiri the following month.[21]

I find it curious that more attacks have not been claimed by AQSP and Ansar al Jihad. It is possible that the group is working in concert with one of the other jihadist organizations in the Sinai.

The Muhammad Jamal Network (MJN)

Muhammad Jamal, who was first trained by al-Qaeda in the late 1980s, was released from prison in 2011 and quickly got back to work. Jamal, who has long been a subordinate to Ayman Zawahiri, became so prolific that his operation was eventually designated by both the U.S. Government and the United Nations.[22] Those designations make it clear that that the MJN operates as part of al-Qaeda's international network. The State Department revealed that Jamal has "established links with terrorists in Europe." In addition to al-Qaeda's senior leadership, the MJN has strong ties to al-Qaeda in the Arabian Peninsula (AQAP) and al-Qaeda in the Islamic Maghreb (AQIM).

Jamal was re-arrested in late 2012. Egyptian authorities discovered on a seized laptop that he had been communicating directly with Ayman Zawahiri.[23] Jamal mentions in the letters that he sent an emissary to meet with Zawahiri after he was blocked from traveling abroad. Jamal claims to have trained several Yemenis who went on to form AQAP and says that AQAP has provided financing for his operations. Jamal writes that he has established training camps in both eastern Libya and the Sinai.

Jamal tells Zawahiri that he formed "groups for us inside Sinai," which is an especially interesting revelation given that some jihadist groups there have openly proclaimed their allegiance to al-Qaeda. He also describes the Sinai as the "the next confrontation arena with the Jews and the Americans." In addition to the Sinai, counterterrorism investigations have revealed that Jamal was a leader of the so-called "Nasr City cell" in Cairo and that his network operates elsewhere in Egypt.

As with al-Qaeda in the Sinai Peninsula (AQSP), I find it curious that the MJN has not claimed any attacks inside Egypt. Jamal's letters reveal that he has procured a significant amount of arms at great expense, including rockets, from Libya and has transported them into the Sinai. Who is using these arms today? What are Jamal's operatives, many of whom remain at-large, doing today?

I surmise it is likely that the MJN is cooperating with other jihadist groups in the Sinai.

Mujahideen Shura Council in the Environs of Jerusalem (MSC)

The MSC operates in both Gaza and the Sinai. The MSC claimed responsibility for a June 18, 2012, cross-border attack in Israel.[24] One Israeli civilian was killed during the attack, which targeted construction workers building a security fence. The group identified an Egyptian and a Saudi as the lead attackers. The MSC dedicated the raid to Osama bin Laden and made its adherence to al-Qaeda's ideology unmistakable.[25] "We announce the formation of the Mujahideen Shura Council in the Environs of Jerusalem, as a base for jihadist work . . . to be part of the global project that aims to re-establish the Caliphate," the group announced in its video claiming responsibility for the attack.[26] "To the Jews, the enemies of Allah, we say: you should know, you infidels, that the future is different from the past . . . The time of negotiations and compromises is over," one MSC member said in the video.[27]

---

[20] Bill Roggio, "Ansar al Jihad in the Sinai Peninsula announces formation," *The Long War Journal,* December 22, 2011. *(http://www.longwarjournal.org/archives/2011/12/ansar_al_jihad_in_th.php)*

[21] Bill Roggio, "Ansar al Jihad swears allegiance to al Qaeda's emir," *The Long War Journal,* January 24, 2012. *(http://www.longwarjournal.org/archives/2012/01/ansar_al_jihad_-swear.php)*

[22] The State Department's announcement of the designation can be found here: *http://www.state.gov/r/pa/prs/ps/2013/10/215171.htm.* The UN's designation can be found here: *http://www.un.org/News/Press/docs/2013/sc11154.doc.htm.*

[23] Thomas Joscelyn, "Communications with Ayman al Zawahiri highlighted in 'Nasr City cell' case," *The Long War Journal,* February 10, 2013. *(http://www.longwarjournal.org/archives/2013/02/communications_with.php)*

[24] Thomas Joscelyn, "Al Qaeda-linked group claims responsibility for attack in Israel," *The Long War Journal,* June 19, 2012. *(http://www.longwarjournal.org/archives/2012/06/al_qaeda-linked_grou.php)*

[25] Ibid.

[26] "Unknown Islamists Claim Border Attack on Israel," *NOW Lebanon* (with *Agence France Presse*), June 19, 2012.

[27] Ibid.

Months later, the MSC released a martyrdom video praising the lead Egyptian in the June 2012 attack. The MSC's advertisement for the video portrayed him as an al-Qaeda martyr, similar to lead 9/11 hijacker Mohammed Atta and al-Qaeda ideologue Anwar al-Awlaki.[28] Also featured in the advertisement was Ahmed Ashush, the long-time ally of the Zawahiri brothers. In a separate video released on July 27, 2012, the MSC again claimed responsibility for the attack and said it was "a gift to our brothers in al Qaeda and Sheikh Zawahiri," as well as retaliation for the death of Osama bin Laden.[29] The MSC referred to Zawahiri as "our sheikh" and said it was "continuing with our pledge of allegiance on the path of jihad."

Al-Qaeda in the Arabian Peninsula (AQAP) in the Sinai

Citing "American officials," *The New York Times* recently reported that AQAP "has regular contact with jihadist groups in Lebanon and in the Sinai Peninsula."[30] This is not surprising given that AQAP help establish Muhammad Jamal's operations in the Sinai and elsewhere. Numerous published reports point to the presence of a significant number of Yemeni militants in the Sinai. It is likely that many of them are working on behalf of AQAP, which has also established a presence in Libya.

In August 2012, CNN reported that ten "Yemeni militants" had "infiltrated Egyptian soil two months ago and trained local Jihadi cells in the Sinai Peninsula."[31] CNN cited a "senior security official associated with Egypt's North Sinai's border guards" as the source for this revelation. This anonymous official said intelligence reports showed the Yemenis "were in communication with Jihadist cells in Al Mukataa, a remote area south of Sheikh Zuweid in Northern Sinai." CNN also cited two Bedouin leaders who were aware of the Yemeni militants' presence in the Sinai. One of these local Bedouins said that the Yemenis had been smuggled into the Sinai from Sudan.

In early September 2013, the *Associated Press* reported that the Sinai "has seen an influx of foreign fighters the past two months, including several hundred Yemenis."[32] The AP also reported that a Yemeni suspected of serving Ramzi Mowafi, the aforementioned head of AQSP, had been arrested. Three months later, in December 2013, a journalist for *Al-Monitor* published his account of an interview with a powerful tribesman in the Sinai who said that Libyans, Palestinians, and Yemenis were all operating in the Sinai.[33] "There are around 1,000 al Qaeda fighters here in the Sinai Peninsula, operating under the different groups, and a lot of them are foreigners," the tribal leader claimed. (Estimates of the number of fighters vary greatly.) He also said that several of the major jihadist groups "coordinate and sometimes run shared operations" and they "are affiliated to al Qaeda in one way or another." In early January 2013, the *Daily Beast* reported that "Western officials believe that foreign jihadis, possibly from Yemen and Somalia, are among the several hundred extremists operating" in the Sinai close to the Israeli border.[34]

ANSAR JERUSALEM (ANSAR BAYT AL-MAQDIS)

Ansar Jerusalem is the most prolific of the Sinai-based jihadist organizations. In recent months, its operations have become more daring and sophisticated. And its

---

[28] Thomas Joscelyn, "Egyptian involved in cross-border attack on Israel portrayed as al Qaeda 'martyr'," *The Long War Journal's Threat Matrix*, February 8, 2013. *(http://www.longwarjournal.org/threat-matrix/archives/2013/02/egyptian_involved_in_cross-bor.php)*

[29] Bill Roggio, "Mujahideen Shura Council calls attack in Israel a 'gift' to Zawahiri and al-Qaeda 'brothers'," *The Long War Journal*, July 30, 2012. *(http://www.longwarjournal.org/archives/2012/07/egyptian_jihadist_gr.php)* A translation of the video was provided by the SITE Intelligence Group.

[30] Robert F. Worth and Eric Schmitt, "Jihadist Groups Gain in Turmoil Across Middle East," *The New York Times*, December 3, 2013. *(http://www.nytimes.com/2013/12/04/world/middleeast/jihadist-groups-gain-in-turmoil-across-middle-east.html?pagewanted=2&_r=1&hp-&pagewanted=all&)*

[31] Mohamed Fadel Fahmy, "Official: Yemeni militants infiltrated Egypt before Rafah attack," CNN.com, August 17, 2012. *http://www.cnn.com/2012/08/17/world/meast/egypt-yemen-militants/*

[32] "Local, foreign Islamic militants turn Egypt's Sinai [into] a new front for jihad," *Associated Press*, September 3, 2013. *(http://www.foxnews.com/world/2013/09/03/local-foreign-islamic-militants-turn-egypt-sinai-new-front-for-jihad/)*

[33] Mohannad Sabry, "Al-Qaeda emerges amid Egypt's turmoil," *Al-Monitor*, December 4, 2013. *(http://www.al-monitor.com/pulse/originals/2013/12/al-qaeda-egypt-sinai-insurgency-growing-influence.html)*

[34] Alastair Beach, "In the North Sinai, Jihadis Stand Down the Egyptian Government," *The Daily Beast*, January 6, 2013. *(http://www.thedailybeast.com/articles/2013/01/06/in-the-north-sinai-jihadis-stand-down-the-egyptian-government.html)*

attacks have stretched into the heart of mainland Egypt. Noteworthy attacks by the group include: A complex multi-stage assault in August 2011 that left eight Israelis and several Egyptians dead, successful and unsuccessful attacks on Egyptian officials (including car bombings), and the downing of an Egyptian military helicopter in late January. The attack on the helicopter involved a shoulder-fired missile, which indicates that the group's capabilities have greatly increased since its inception.

Little is known about Ansar Jerusalem's inner workings, however. We do not know, based on open-source information, the extent of Ansar Jerusalem's connections to al-Qaeda's international network. Little is known about the identities and biographies of the group's founders or current leaders. Nor do we know how many members the group has, or how it is financed.[35] Ansar Jerusalem's precise ties to other jihadist groups in Egypt, including the recently-formed Ajnad Misr, are also murky. (Ansar Jerusalem refers to Ajnad Misr as "our brothers.")

Thus, counterterrorism analysts cannot know for certain the extent of the group's operational ties (if any) to al-Qaeda's senior leadership or al-Qaeda's official branches. This does not mean that such ties do not exist. In the past, al-Qaeda has groomed organizations and so-called affiliates without recognizing them, at least at first, as formal al-Qaeda entities.[36] It could be the case, therefore, that Ansar Jerusalem is already acting as a clandestine arm al-Qaeda. We just do not know for certain one way or the other.

Late last year, Egyptian officials alleged that a long-time Egyptian Islamic Jihad (EIJ) leader named Ahmed Salama Mabrouk plays a leading role in Ansar Jerusalem.[37] If true, then this is a major red flag. Mabrouk has been a subordinate to Ayman Zawahiri for decades. He also served al-Qaeda after the EIJ became a part of Osama bin Laden's joint venture. After his release from prison in Egypt, Mabrouk starred at Ansar al Sharia Egypt events alongside Mohammed Zawahiri.

With those uncertainties in mind, a survey of the available evidence shows that Ansar Jerusalem is, at a minimum, pursing al-Qaeda's agenda and al-Qaeda's senior leadership approves of the organization.

Ayman Zawahiri has repeatedly praised Ansar Jerusalem's operations. And the group routinely references senior al-Qaeda leaders in its propaganda videos. This is one reason why the group is commonly described as "al-Qaeda-inspired" in the press. The group has adopted al-Qaeda's tactics, including suicide bombings. And there are various other threads of evidence pointing to Ansar Jerusalem's international ties.

My informed hunch is that Ansar Jerusalem has, at the very least, coordinated its activities with parts of al-Qaeda's international network. Below, I summarize some of the evidence connecting Ansar Jerusalem to the al-Qaeda network.

Propaganda distributed through al-Qaeda's channels

Ansar Jerusalem distributes its propaganda through al-Qaeda's official on-line channels. In October 2013, the group issued a statement denying "any connection to any account on social networking pages," adding that "the only source of our statements and productions are the jihadi forums from al Fajr Media Center (Shumukh al Islam Network and al Fida' Islamic Network)."[38] Al Fajr is al-Qaeda's propaganda distribution arm, while the other two sites are al-Qaeda-accredited. Ansar Jerusalem's messages are often "stickied" at the top of Shumukh, showing that they are considered important by the administrators on al-Qaeda's top websites.[39]

Ansar Jerusalem frequently includes clips of al-Qaeda's top leaders in its videos. Clips of Osama bin Laden and Abu Yahya al Libi (a top al-Qaeda operative killed

---

[35] Undoubtedly, U.S. intelligence officials have additional, Classified information on Ansar Jerusalem.

[36] For instance, Osama bin Laden instructed Shabaab, which became a formal affiliate of al-Qaeda in 2012, to hide its organizational ties to al-Qaeda. Jabhat al Nusrah hid its allegiance to Ayman Zawahiri at first and was branded in such a manner as to disguise its al-Qaeda's role in its creation. Senior al-Qaeda operatives have been leaders within organizations that are not officially recognized as al-Qaeda entities, such as Ahrar al Sham in Syria. And al-Qaeda employs multiple brands to increase its influence. In Yemen, for example, al-Qaeda in the Arabian Peninsula (AQAP) began using the name Ansar al Sharia. Other al-Qaeda-linked organizations have also adopted the same name, including Ansar al Sharia Egypt, which is headed by jihadists loyal to Ayman Zawahiri.

[37] See: *http://www.shorouknews.com/news/view.aspx?cdate=22122013&id=84d10683-9c61-44fc-a97a-08d4b8c3f954.*

[38] SITE Intelligence Group, "Ansar Jerusalem Claims Bombing at Military Intelligence HQ in Ismailia," October 21, 2013. The group repeated this statement about his distribution channels on January 24, 2014.

[39] BBC Monitoring, "Web monitoring report for 8–10 September 2012," September 10, 2012.

in June 2012) discussing martyrdom were included in a video honoring a member of the group who had participated in the August 2011 attacks in Eilat.[40] Another video, honoring a suicide bomber who blew himself up inside the South Sinai Security Directorate on October 7, 2013, included an audio clip of Ayman Zawahiri.[41] Still another video featured a clip of deceased al-Qaeda in Iraq leader Abu Musab al-Zarqawi.[42]

In January 2014, Ayman Zawahiri directed part of a message "to our people in Sinai." A clip from an Ansar Jerusalem video, showing a funeral for some of its members, was included in this section of Zawahiri's message.[43]

Ansar Jerusalem's rocket attacks on Israel, gas pipeline bombings, and other operations

Ansar Jerusalem has repeatedly launched rockets at Israel and attacked the Arish-Ashkelon pipeline. In an August 2011 audio message, Zawahiri praised the gas pipeline attacks, which Ansar Jerusalem has claimed as its own. "Not only does the siege of Gaza continue, but also continues the provision of Israel with Egyptian gas at prices lower than the market price," Zawahiri said in the video. "Were gas sold to Israel at a price higher than the market price, it would be a crime. What can [you] then say about this compound crime?!" Zawahiri continued: "I here commend the heroes who blew up the gas pipeline to Israel. I ask Allah to reward them for their heroic act, for they have expressed the anger of the Islamic Ummah against this continuing crime from the reign of Hosni Mubarak to the rule of the Military Council . . . ".[44]

Two months later, in a video released in October 2011, Zawahiri lauded Ansar Jerusalem's attacks on Eilat, Israel. Ansar Jerusalem claimed responsibility for the attacks in a statement released on September 7. The attacks were carried out on August 18 and killed eight Israelis. "And just as I congratulated our people in Libya for their great victory," Zawahiri said in his video, "I congratulate our mujahideen brothers who carried out the two Eilat operations." Zawahiri claimed that one "of the gains of [Ansar Jerusalem's] operation was exposing the treason of the ruling military council, which was quick to send its troops to chase [Ansar Jerusalem's terrorists] in order to protect Israel's security, and then begging from Israel to increase the forces in the area so as to pursue Israel's enemies."[45]

Zawahiri has trumpeted Ansar Jerusalem's gas pipeline attacks on multiple other occasions. In a June 2012 video, Zawahiri heaped praise on the group, calling Ansar Jerusalem members "brave lions" and saying that they should serve as the "guiding example" for Muslims. "I take this opportunity to salute the brave lions, the mujahideen, who blew up the gas pipe to Israel for the thirteenth time," Zawahiri said in the video. Al-Qaeda's emir continued: "May Allah salute you as lions who do not let justice go in vain, or accept humiliation, and do not accept for the fortunes of the Muslims to be given to their enemies. Therefore, go on the path of Jihad and count what you meet in the Cause of Allah, who does not let the reward of His workers go to waste. Be the guiding example for every free, honorable person who is passionate for Islam in the Egypt of Islam and jihad."[46]

In July 2012, Ansar Jerusalem issued a video claiming 13 attacks on the pipeline. Several clips of Ayman Zawahiri were played throughout the video. The clips show Zawahiri praising the pipeline bombings on at least three separate occasions. In one scene, terrorists are shown planting an explosive device at the pipeline while an audio clip from Zawahiri is played in the background: "Just giving gas to Israel is

---

[40] SITE Intelligence Group, "Ansar Jerusalem Video Eulogizes Fighter, Shows Spy Interrogation," November 7, 2012.

[41] SITE Intelligence Group, "Ansar Jerusalem Releases Video on Suicide Bombing at South Sinai Security Directorate," November 19, 2013. The video also includes a clip of the deceased leader of the Islamic State of Iraq, Abu Omar al Baghdadi.

[42] SITE Intelligence Group, "Ansar Jerusalem Releases Video of Training, Attacking Egyptian Soldiers," December 2, 2013. Also shown in the video is the spokesman for the Islamic State of Iraq and the Sham (ISIS).

[43] David Barnett, "Zawahiri's message 'to our people in Sinai'," *The Long War Journal, Threat Matrix* blog, January 27, 2014. *(http://www.longwarjournal.org/threat-matrix/archives/2014/01/zawahiris_message_to_our_peopl.php)*

[44] SITE Intelligence Group, "Zawahiri Charges America with Hijacking the Egyptian Revolution," August 8, 2011.

[45] SITE Intelligence Group, "Zawahiri Praises Libyan Rebels, Eilat Attackers; Urges Algerians to Revolt," October 11, 2011. Zawahiri further claimed that the United States had "commissioned" Egypt's ruling military council. His statement was recorded sometime in August or September 2011, meaning it could have been recorded either before or contemporaneous with Ansar Jerusalem's claim of responsibility for the Eilat attacks.

[46] SITE Intelligence Group, "Zawahiri Demands Shariah in Egypt, Remarks on Razing of Bin Laden House," June 17, 2012.

a crime even if it is for the market price, so imagine that it is below the market price. Thus, it is a crime by Mubarak that is continued by the ruling military council." As the bomb explodes, Zawahiri continues: "The greeting goes to the heroes who blew up the gas pipeline and who represent the dignity of the Egyptian people. May Allah bless them, until they see the Islamic Caliphate ruling over the countries of Islam. I ask Allah to grant them patience and determination, and to reward them in the best way in this life and the hereafter." Subsequent clips of Zawahiri in Ansar Jerusalem's July 2012 video show the al-Qaeda master praising the gas pipeline attacks after the "tenth" and "twelfth" such attacks.[47]

Used the video "Innocence of Muslims" as a pretext for terrorism

Ansar Jerusalem has claimed responsibility for a cross-border raid that killed an Israeli soldier on September 21, 2012.[48] Three jihadists were also killed in the attack, which was dubbed the "raid of punishment." Ansar Jerusalem claimed the assault was retaliation for the video "Innocence of Muslims" and necessary "to discipline those insulting the beloved Prophet."[49]

As I've reported, multiple known al-Qaeda actors seized upon the anti-Islam video as a pretext to justify protests and assaults on U.S. diplomatic facilities beginning on September 11, 2012.[50] Ansar Jerusalem's use of the video to justify an attack in Israel is a good example of how the video was used as a pretext, not a true motivation, by jihadists allied with al-Qaeda. Ansar Jerusalem blamed Jews for producing the film, even though there was no Jewish involvement in its production. And, in reality, Ansar Jerusalem did not need the video justify its attacks as it struck Israel both before and long after the video became widely known.

On January 11, 2013, Ansar Jerusalem released a video in which it once again claimed that the attack in Israel was in response to Innocence of Muslims. The group cited Osama bin Laden as saying, "If the freedom of your expression has no limit, then your chests should bear the freedom of our actions."[51] This quote, or a similar one, was used by jihadists with known al-Qaeda ties to justify the protest-turned-assault on the U.S. Embassy in Cairo on September 11, 2012.[52] Indeed, the Ansar Jerusalem video contains footage from that pro-al-Qaeda event. The video also contains an audio clip of Abu Musab al-Zarqawi, the former leader of al-Qaeda in Iraq who was killed in 2006.[53]

Threatened retaliation for Israel's killing of two top terrorists in Gaza

On October 15, 2012, Ansar Jerusalem threatened retaliation against Israel for the killing of two jihadist leaders, Hisham al Saedni (a.k.a. Abu al Walid al Maqdisi) and Ashraf Sabah (a.k.a. Abu al Bara'a al Maqdisi). Al Saedni, an Egyptian, was the founder and leader of the Tawhid and Jihad Group, which is, at a minimum, al-Qaeda-inspired.

Al Saedni reportedly fought with al-Qaeda in Iraq. Although he was based in Gaza and even detained for a time by Hamas, the Israeli military accused al Saedni of planning operations from inside the Sinai. His biography shows, therefore, that al Saedni had been a transnational terrorist throughout his career and it is possible that he cooperated with Ansar Jerusalem. There are numerous other accounts pointing to collusion between Ansar Jerusalem and terrorists based in, or traveling to, Gaza.[54]

---

[47] SITE Intelligence Group, "Ansar Jerusalem Releases Video of Bombing Arish-Ashkelon Pipeline," July 24, 2012. Like other Ansar Jerusalem messages, the video was released on al-Qaeda's Shumukh al-Islam forum.

[48] Bill Roggio, "Ansar Jerusalem claims attack on Israeli troops in the Sinai," *The Long War Journal,* September 23, 2012. *(http://www.longwarjournal.org/archives/2012/09/ansar_jerusalem_clai.php)*

[49] "Egypt jihadi groups say behind deadly Israeli border attack," *Al-Masry Al-Youm Online,* September 23, 2012.

[50] See: Thomas Joscelyn, "Al Qaeda Lives," *The Weekly Standard,* December 24, 2012. *(http://www.weeklystandard.com/articles/al-qaeda-lives_666594.html)*

[51] SITE Intelligence Group, "Ansar Jerusalem Releases Video on 9/2012 Cross-Border Attack," January 14, 2013.

[52] Thomas Joscelyn, "CIA Warned of 'Jihadist' Threat to Cairo Embassy," *The Weekly Standard,* May 15, 2013. *(http://www.weeklystandard.com/blogs/cia-warned-jihadist-threat-cairo-embassy_724570.html)*

[53] SITE Intelligence Group, January 14, 2013.

[54] Just recently, Israeli forces claimed to have killed a terrorist in the Gaza Strip who had "cooperated" with Ansar Jerusalem. See: Elior Levy, "IAF strikes Gaza; Israel says member of Global Jihad wounded," ynetnews.com, February 9, 2014. *(http://www.ynetnews.com/articles/0,7340,L-4486138,00.html)* Egyptian security officials have also claimed that Ansar Jerusalem members have escaped security operations in the Sinai by fleeing to Gaza. See: "Ansar Bayt al-Maqdis members escape to Gaza, Marsa Matrouh," *Al-Masry Al-Youm,* September 12, 2013.

It is possible that the Tawhid and Jihad Group is more than merely inspired by al-Qaeda as well. Ayman Zawahiri released a eulogy for al Saedni, praising him as "our brother." Zawahiri also cited al-Qaeda's guidelines, which was named as a "Document for Supporting Islam," and said that al-Qaeda had called on Muslims "to unite under the word Tawhid." Thus, Zawahiri implicitly connected al Saedni and his group to al-Qaeda's plans. Indeed, al Saedni was working to unite jihadist groups in Gaza under one banner. The praise for al Saedni from both al-Qaeda and Ansar Jerusalem is yet another example of how the two count the same terrorists among their "brothers." Both al Saedni and Sabah were reportedly leaders in the Mujahideen Shura Council in the Environs of Jerusalem as well.

Assassination attempt on Egyptian Interior Minister

Ansar Jerusalem has claimed responsibility for the September 5, 2013 assassination attempt on Egyptian Interior Minister Mohammed Ibrahim. On October 26, 2013, the group released a video dedicated to the suicide bomber responsible for the operation, a former major in the Egyptian army named Walid Badr. The video is framed by an audio clip from Ayman Zawahiri at the beginning and a video clip of Zawahiri at the end.[55]

In the closing scene Zawahiri says that the conflict in Egypt is "a struggle between political parties, but a struggle between Crusaders and Zionists on one side and Islam on the other side."[56]

Badr's story demonstrates how Ansar Jerusalem is connected to the al-Qaeda-led global jihadist network. The video by Ansar Jerusalem celebrating his "martyrdom" says he traveled to Afghanistan and participated "with his brothers in deterring the Crusader campaign against the proud land of Khorasan." This is a reference to the America-led campaign in Afghanistan that began in late 2001. Badr attempted to fight in Iraq as well, but he "was arrested in Iran, where he was put in prison for about a year," before he returned to Egypt. At some point, he traveled to Syria to fight Bashar al Assad's regime, only to return to Egypt once again and become a suicide bomber.[57] This sequence of events shows that Badr managed to fight in three different theaters (Afghanistan, Syria, and Egypt), making him a global jihadist.

There are still additional details in Badr's story that connect him and Ansar Jerusalem to the al-Qaeda network. Egyptian officials alleged that he was trained by the Muhammad Jamal Network in one of its Libyan camps.[58] And, in late October 2013, Egyptian security sources arrested Nabil al Maghraby, whom they described simply as "a key al-Qaeda operative."[59] Al Maghraby is one of the old school jihadists let out of prison in the wake of the Egyptian revolution. He had been imprisoned for the 1981 assassination of Egyptian president Anwar Sadat, but was freed by a presidential pardon from Mohamed Morsi in 2012. Egyptian authorities described al Maghraby as "a close associate" of Badr.

Thank you again for inviting me to testify today. I look forward to answering your questions.

Mr. KING. Thank you, Mr. Joscelyn.

Our next witness is Mr. Mohamed Elmenshawy, who is a resident scholar and a director of languages at the regional study program at the Middle East Institute.

Mr. Elmenshawy, we certainly look forward to your testimony, and you are recognized. Thank you.

(http://www.egyptindependent.com/news/ansar-bayt-al-maqdis-members-escape-gaza-marsa-matrouh)

[55] SITE Intelligence Group, "Ansar Jerusalem Releases Video on Assassination Attempt on Egyptian Interior Minister," October 27, 2013. Also included in the video is a clip of a spokesman from the Islamic State of Iraq and the Sham (ISIS), which was then a branch of al-Qaeda but has since been disowned by al-Qaeda's senior leadership.

[56] Liam Stack and Robert Mackey, "Egyptian Jihadists Cite Zawahiri in Video Claiming Responsibility for Cairo Attack," *The New York Times, The Lede blog,* October 29. 2013. *(http://thelede.blogs.nytimes.com/2013/10/29/egyptian-jihadists-cite-zawahiri-in-video-claiming-responsibility-for-cairo-attack/?_php=true&_type=blogs&_r=0)*

[57] SITE Intelligence Group, October 27, 2013.

[58] "Jihadists see Sinai as 'next frontier' in war against U.S., Israel," UPI, October 30, 2013. *(http://www.upi.com/Top_News/Special/2013/10/30/Jihadists-see-Sinai-as-next-frontier-in-war-against-US-Israel/UPI-44931383144187/)*

[59] "Egypt arrests al Qaeda militant previously jailed for Sadat murder," *Reuters,* October 29, 2013. *(http://www.reuters.com/article/2013/10/29/us-egypt-militants-idUSBRE99S0WP2013-1029)*

STATEMENT OF MOHAMED ELMENSHAWY, RESIDENT SCHOLAR AT THE MIDDLE EASTERN INSTITUTE

Mr. ELMENSHAWY. Thank you, Mr. Chairman, and Ranking Member of the committee, for inviting me to speak about this important topic today.

It is rather demoralizing that we are having this conversation exactly today, February 11. Actually 3 years ago, exactly as Steven mentioned, millions of Egyptians celebrated the resignation of former President Hosni Mubarak after 30 years of autocratic rule.

For a moment, some believed that forcing such a strong regime to surrender to the desire of nonviolent protestors meant a huge setback for al-Qaeda and other militant groups' ideologies that advocate violence and use of terrorism as only tool for change. Yet, the events in Egypt, however, continue to unfold.

The first-ever democratically-elected president of the country's history was brought to office later on. Exactly a year later, on June 30 last year, massive protestors flooded the streets of Egypt asking for early retirement, and that triggered—triggered the military to intervene and oust the President on July 3. This is the context in which we are examining our topic today.

I would like to address three major indicators that affect the counterterrorism efforts in Egypt: First, the potential for political revolution for Egypt's existing political crisis; second, the increased trend to resort to violence; and the perception of the United States and its role in these events.

Egypt, as we know now, they have no potential for political solution—resolution at this moment. We have witnessing huge polarization in Egyptian social and political forces. It is a zero-sum game between the two competing bodies of Egypt, the military and the Muslim Brotherhood. Meanwhile, the security solution continue to gain upper hand, thus culminating by designing the Muslim Brotherhood as a terrorist group in December 25 last year.

Currently, the majority of the Muslim Brotherhood's leadership are behind bars and awaiting trial and the President himself is facing serious charges, including espionage. If convicted, he would face capital punishment.

Some Egyptian independent sources indicate that civilians killed since the ousting of Morsi reach number 2,421 as well as 174 police officer and 70 from the military, in addition to 11 journalists in this 7 months.

Second important issue I would like to call—to talk about today is the resort to violence by all political forces in Egypt. Where the political avenues is closed, there is trend to use violence by al-Qaeda militant group and other people especially they use recently.

It is very important to distinguish between the two emerging form of militants in Egypt. One is the terrorist fight operating in Sinai, especially the Ansar Bayt al Maqdis—and in Sinai it is multi-dimensional group that operating using violence, and some of them are local Bedouin who are fighting marginalization by the Cairo government and some of them extensive organized crime—criminals who are doing smuggling and trafficking of men and woman and weapons—and most importantly, in Sinai, of course, as our colleague said, the Ansar Bayt al Maqdis, which in Arabic is

Companion of Jerusalem, which has been the champion of violence in Sinai in last few months.

In talking about these people, they have, in last 2 months, changed their tactic dramatically. They moved their operation outside Sinai to, we believe, an area in Egypt, in Cairo, in Dakahlia and in Mansoura and Ismailiyya and others, and they show some sophistication of this capability by downing a military helicopter a few weeks ago and killing the 5 crew members.

In addition to this violent militant group, there is a new trend of violence by use of the revolution. We have a group called "Walaa'," which is "burn," and Molotov Movement, which claimed responsibility for burning a lot of cars and bikers of the military and the police officers.

How this affects the United States force. Within this brutalized society in Egypt now, the only issue that unites Egyptians is blaming United States for lots gone wrong.

Islamists believe Washington supported the coup against President Morsi, while pro-military Egyptians believe Washington has a special relation with the Brotherhood that was instrumental in installing Morsi as President.

Some of this negativity towards the United States is result of conspiracy theories based on unsubstantiated accusations that are propagated by sensational media, which is widely influential in Egypt today.

A lot of claims, which are ridiculous in some sense, are all over Egypt media, such as the United States wants to divide Egypt into small states and Brotherhood takes its orders directly from the White House and from President Obama.

This negativity perception of the United States so far doesn't translate to any direct threat to U.S. interest in the region. These different violent trends I described, including al-Qaeda and Sinai and others, have focused on hard Egyptian targets, mainly military and police so far.

But there is no doubt, this current popular mood in Eqypt towards the United States and lack of political openness is creating an environment less hospitable to the United States in the region.

My assessment is there is no reason to believe at this stage that there is an imminent risk of violence within the United States emanating from its current position in Egypt; however, I believe that the deadlock of Egyptian politics today make it very difficult to cooperate with other countries in countering terrorism.

I will be happy to answer any question.

[The prepared statement of Mr. Elmenshawy follows:]

PREPARED STATEMENT OF MOHAMED ELMENSHAWY

11 FEBRUARY 2014

Mr. Chairman and Members of the subcommittee, thank you very much for inviting me here today to discuss this important issue. It is rather demoralizing that we are having this conversation today. Exactly 3 years ago, millions of Egyptians celebrated the resignation of former president Hosni Mubark after 30 years of autocratic rule.

For a moment, some believed that forcing such a strong regime to surrender to the desire of non-violent protestors meant a huge set-back to al-Qaeda and other groups with militant ideologies that advocate the use terrorism and violence as the only tool for change.

Events in Egypt, however, continued to unfold. After bringing down former President Mubarak, the first-ever democratically-elected president in the country's history was brought to office. Exactly a year later, on June 30, 2013, massive protests flooded the streets calling for early presidential elections and triggering a military intervention that ousted the elected president on July 3.

These events have ushered in a period of unprecedented use of violence by militant groups (especially in Sinai) as well as by the state.

This is the context in which we are examining our question today.

To address it, I will look at three relevant indicators:

(1) The potential for political resolution.
(2) The trends and characteristics of the resort to violence.
(3) The perceptions of the U.S. role in the events.

First: The potential for political resolution.

The potential for political resolution at the moment is in my assessment negligible. While the position of the Egyptian government is centered around accepting the roadmap declared on July 3, the opposition groups led by the Muslim Brotherhood continue to demand the reinstatement of the ousted president. Well-known international efforts led by the European Union, the United States, and some other Arab governments have failed to achieve any rapprochement in these opposing positions.

Meanwhile the security solution continued to gain the upper hand and culminated in the designation of the Muslim Brotherhood as a terrorist organization on the 25th of December 2013. Currently, the majority of the Muslim Brotherhood's leadership is in prison and the ousted president is on trial for a growing list of offences that recently expanded to include espionage. If convicted he faces mandatory capital punishment. Independent figures estimate the total numbers in prison to be thousands from the ranks of the Brotherhood and its sympathizers. The number of civilians killed in confrontations with the security apparatus is estimated to be 2,421, as well as 174 from the police, 70 from the military, and 11 journalists according to independent Egyptian source "Wikithawra".

The recent wave of arrests of journalists and the lack of response to mounting international pressure further illustrate the security bias and the shrinking influence of the moderate voices within the current government. The security approach has been constantly expanding and reaching political activists that were in opposition to the MB government and supportive of the roadmap. It is also expanding to ordinary forms of political activism.

On the other hand, the protests by the Brotherhood and its "Anti-Coup alliance" continue to totally reject the roadmap. Reinstituting the ousted president remains their position.

The potential for political resolution is further hindered by the unparalleled level of social and political polarization. A "zero-sum" attitude is prevalent among all the main players. A poll conducted by Zogby International in September 2013 revealed that 50% of Egyptians want the Brotherhood completely banned from political life. The few political figures from the supporters of the current government who called for reconciliation have faced severe backlash by the media that amounted to character assassination.

Second: The trends and characteristics of the resort to violence.

As political avenues continue to close, the trend towards violence—including by al-Qaeda-style groups—is on a steady rise. Here it is helpful to distinguish between violence emerging out of militant groups in the Sinai Peninsula and the new trend towards violence amongst youth protestors.

Militant presence in Sinai is not new. From 2004 through 2007, a wave of terrorist attacks was carried out against tourist resorts in southern Sinai that killed about 200 people. Violence in Sinai is multifaceted. Some is carried out by local Bedouin groups against the central government in retaliation for marginalization and heavy-handed security practices. Some is linked to the Arab-Israeli conflict and aims to undermine Egypt's peace treaty with Israel. Other violence is linked to extensive organized criminal activities including drug and human trafficking and smuggling of weapons. Finally, most of the violence is the result of Qaeda-style militant groups taking refuge in Sinai because of its topography that defies policing.

After the temporary collapse of the police force on 28 January 2011, violence increased significantly in Sinai as illustrated by the regular attacks on the gas lines transporting gas to Jordan and Israel and police stations.

Since the ousting of president Morsi, a group called the Ansar Beit Al Maqdes Arabic for "Companions of Jerusalem" came to prominence with a constant stream of attacks inside Sinai against military and policy targets, which resulted in the death of dozens policemen and military personnel.

Since November 2013, we should note two emerging trends in the violence by "Companions of Jerusalem" group: They have begun to carry out operations in the densely-populated areas of the Nile Delta and Cairo. This included the bombing of the Security Headquarter in Mansoura on December 24, which led to the designation of the MB as a terrorist group the next day. It also included a number of attempted and successful assassinations of senior police figures, such as the attempted assassination of the Minister of Interior on September 5.

The other trend is the increased sophistication and capabilities of the group in Sinai. This was clearly illustrated when the group claimed responsibility for downing a military helicopter in Sinai in late January killing all 5 crewmembers on board. Based on a video released by the group purporting to show the attack, the militants used a shoulder-fired missile which required serious training and are considered to be more advanced than weapons systems previously seen among militant groups.

Equally significant is the trend towards the use of violence by youth groups that do not fit the typical profile of militant organizations. The Facebook pages of two unknown groups: Walaa' Arabic for "Burn" and "Molotov Movement" claimed responsibility for some recent attacks against police and military assets. "Walaa'" states on its Facebook page that it is a popular movement aiming to resist the oppressive state. The movement also states that it has no political or religious affiliation. These Facebook-formed groups call for burning and destroying the newly rising "repressive state" by targeting police and military vehicles. The burning of police vehicles has become a daily event in the news in Egypt in recent weeks.

Third: The perceptions of the U.S. role in the events.

It seems that the perception of the United States is the only issue that unites highly-divided Egyptians at this stage. Islamists believe that Washington supported a coup against the elected president, while pro-military Egyptians believe that Washington has a special relationship with the Brotherhood and was instrumental in installing Morsi as president.

The Egyptian public is overwhelmingly negative toward the United States and few Egyptians say it is important to have a strong bilateral relationship with Washington. More than half of the public thinks U.S. financial assistance has a negative impact on Egypt.

A poll conducted last summer by Pew Research showed that 81% of Egyptians have expressed an unfavorable opinion about the United States with only 16% favorable. Negative perceptions of the United States have been consistent in recent years. These numbers reflect attitudes that are more negative today than during much of President George W. Bush's time in office.

According to the same poll, few in Egypt find having a good relationship with the United States a priority. Only 24% say it is important for Egypt to have a strong partnership with America, while 9% think it is very important. Nearly 7 in 10 (69%) say a good bilateral relationship is not very important or not at all important.

Some of the negativity towards the United States, to be sure, is the result of conspiracy theories and unsubstantiated accusations that are propagated by sensational media. They include claims such as the "the United States wants to divide Egypt" into several states; that "Morsi was an American spy"; and that "the Brotherhood takes its orders directly from Obama".

Conversely, some Islamists retain anger against the United States for tolerating the repressive tactics of Mubarak's regime. Currently, almost all Islamists believe America has abandoned Morsi and "electoral legitimacy" after his July 3 overthrow. Of course, many also still retain the belief that the United States is against any form of Islamism by default. They see the recent policy on events in Egypt as proof.

So far this negative perception of the U.S. role has not translated into violence against U.S. interests. The different violent trends that I described today, including al-Qaeda-related groups, have focused so far on "hard" Egyptian targets mostly linked to the security apparatus. There is no doubt however that the current popular mood in Egypt and the lack of genuine political openness is creating an environment less hospitable to the United States in the region. It is my assessment that there is no reason to believe at this stage that there is an imminent risk of violence within the United States emanating from the current situation in Egypt.

Thank you, Mr. Chairman, for giving me the opportunity to testify before your committee today. I look forward to answering any questions you or your colleagues may have.

Mr. KING. Thank you very much, all of you, for your testimony.

There is many new names and groups being mentioned. I would just state for the record that Ansar Bayt al Maqdes, ABM, and

Ansar Jerusalem are the same organization. They're just different terms, same organization, just to get them in the record.

It seems there is a consensus that there is an emerging threat there, something we—something we have to be very concerned about. This is a fertile area and, ultimately, it could be used as an attack against the homeland or just an attack against our interests in the Middle East.

I would ask each of you actually two questions, and you can just go around among yourselves.

First of all, do you believe that other intelligence agencies in the region who are allied with us share this concern that you have—we have?

Second, what advice would you give to the United States in its dealings with Egypt to effectively move against these groups?

We'll start with Dr. Cook and go across.

Mr. COOK. Thank you very much. Those are two important questions.

I think the relevant and most important intelligence agency in the region is, obviously, the Israelis. As I mentioned in my testimony and as I have submitted in my written testimony, Israelis have expressed concern about the deterioration of security in the Sinai for quite some time and are particularly concerned about the turn of events there; so, I think that they do share the assessment.

They are primarily concerned with the destabilization of a country of almost 90 million people on their border, but I think that they see a broader view of it in the same way that my colleague Mr. Joscelyn sees it, as an emerging threat that has the potential to not only threaten them, but to threaten the United States as well.

In terms of what the United States can do to be helpful for the Egyptians—this is something that I started to get into in my remarks—I think that we have had a robust debate here in Washington about how best to help Egypt become a more democratic country.

I think the trajectory of Egyptian politics is clearly an authoritarian one, not a democratic one. Suspending or delaying military aid isn't going to make Egypt more democratic at this moment. It's also not going to make Egypt less unstable. It is also not going to help Egypt's security situation.

We need to work very closely with the Egyptian armed forces who, as I said, have been reluctant to rethink their doctrine for 21st Century threats, but have been more open to it more recently.

In my written testimony, I have specific recommendations for this, but I think that the only way—the only way that the Egyptians will really listen to the United States in this area is if we reassure them that we do stand with them.

The proposals to suspend aid, to delay certain important pieces of equipment, like Apache helicopters, actually do damage to the trust that we have tried to build up between the United States and the Egyptian armed forces over many, many years.

If we were to resume—if we were to resume the aid relationship the way it has been, we do have an opportunity to work with the Egyptians in developing their doctrine in a way that will be more responsive to these threats.

That is not to suggest that this is a—this is an easy situation. I think everybody supports Egypt becoming a democracy. That is a laudable goal. I have written quite a bit about that.

But if we are thinking in the current environment what the United States can do and what our security interests are, it means working with the Egyptian armed forces specifically in countering this threat.

Thank you.

Mr. KING. Mr. Joscelyn.

Mr. JOSCELYN. I think you can tell by press reporting that a number of intelligence agencies around the region and the world are worried about the growing threat, in particular, Israel, as my colleague here says.

Israel is concerned because what is happening in the Sinai is connected with what happens in Gaza. There is movement back and forth, obviously. Israel has come under attack from Council of Jerusalem or ABM a number of occasions.

In August 2011, there was a sort of sophisticated Mumbai-style attack against Israeli tourists and others that, basically—what happened was Israelis then had to chase Egyptian assailants back into Sinai and this created a major problem for Israel because it sparked outrage and protests leading to the Israeli embassy basically being assaulted.

On your latter point—latter question about what we should do about it, I think that what we have to understand is that Ansar Jerusalem, ABM, these groups, they are terrorist organizations, but they are more than that. They are insurgents and they are operating as a low-grade, right now, insurgency.

So Egypt's policies, in terms of combatting them, has to take that in mind in understanding that, if you get too heavy-handed in your tactics, too sort-of cavalier in what you are doing, you can actually feed into what these groups want to do in terms of winning over new recruits.

This is something, as you know, Congressman, that it took the United States a number of years to get right in Iraq and elsewhere to—understanding how to work with local partners to basically counter the threat of these groups.

I think that is really the main issue in the Sinai, is that there are definitely groups that be can embraced by the state there to try and work against these emerging al-Qaeda threats.

Mr. KING. Mr. Elmenshawy.

Mr. ELMENSHAWY. I believe a lot of intelligence agency are interested in what is wrong with Egypt, of course, Israeli in the top, and Arab countries as well, because what is happening in Egypt won't stay in Egypt and they know that for the soft power Egypt enjoy and are still enjoying over the region.

As for the United States, I believe they have big dilemma here. It is very difficult to cooperate with Egyptian government in the current situation because the democratic process imposed by the military is not inclusive to all political forces, especially the Muslim Brotherhood.

The mission of the Brotherhood as terrorist group on December 25 hurts counterterrorism effort because they put them in the same group with real radical militant groups such as Ansar Bayt al Maqdis, which is the focus of everybody today.

Motion the government of Egypt privately and publicly to have a real democratic process that include everybody, include—with concerns to have unity within Egyptian and having the Muslim Brotherhood to be a legal and legitimate player will help counter-terrorism efforts.

But excluding them, it's very golden opportunity to use by al-Qaeda and other militants to recruit angry young Muslim Brotherhood and besides that are members who will find democracy doesn't serve their goal and their aspiration, and they may resort to terrorism and violence.

Besides that, I believe in this atmosphere where United States is blamed by everybody in Egypt, Islamists, pro-military, pro-everybody and, at any action, some of this ridiculously orchestrated, I believe United States should say publicly: We are dealing with the ruler of Egypt. We are not choosing who is in charge. We dealt with Mubarak and with Tantawi, with Morsi, with Sisi, and we are not responsible for whoever in charge of Egypt. We just deal with whoever ends up—had their ballots—the presidential ballots to Egypt and stay away from calling repeatedly in conferences here, we encourage or ask government of Egypt to do X and Y and Z. That should be private, and they should meet, too. Egyptian people, it is clear, we are dealing with whoever in charge. We are not influencing whom you choose.

Mr. KING. Mr. Higgins.

Mr. HIGGINS. Thank you, Mr. Chairman.

You know, just to step back for a moment, you know, the shame here is that, in 2011, during the uprising, in the final days in Tahrir Square, you had 8 million people, 10 percent of the Nation's population, which really represented the largest pro-democracy movement in the history of world.

To have such a disastrous outcome, I think, you know, you can certainly look to the Muslim Brotherhood in their misreading the situation by trying to impose Islamists' identity on Egypt, which is really a nationalist, you know, population. It is 90 percent Sunni, 10 percent Coptic Christian.

So Morsi is thrown out, creates all kinds of instability. Sinai Peninsula, which is very strategic to us because of its close proximity to Gaza, because of its close proximity to Israel, seems to be overtaken by an al-Qaeda-influenced affiliate. Their activity seemed to be spreading to the mainland. They have surface-to-air missile capability or are believed to, which enhances, you know, their threat moving forward.

You know, who is winning this thing? Is the military, in this period of flux, able to keep in check this al-Qaeda affiliate or al-Qaeda-encouraged or -endorsed activity? I mean, what is—what is the situation?

Because there is two—there is two problems here. There is two problems here. You know, one is a failed state in Egypt is disastrous for Israel and the United States. Disastrous.

So, you know, what is being done in the short term to stem this tide of al-Qaeda-influenced activity? You know, right beyond that, you know, what is—what is the way forward in terms of some kind of functioning government that can respect the rights of minorities, that can respect a separation of powers, that gives the people of that country that I think legitimately stood up 3 years ago for the things that we wanted them to embrace?

That is a rule of law, that is minority rights, that is all the things that we value or at least, you know, a semblance of a democracy.

How do we get back to that, I suppose, you know, is the question?

Mr. COOK. Thank you very much, sir.

You raise a number of very interesting and interconnected questions, and I think what I will do is I will answer them in backwards order, if you don't mind.

It strikes me that we are in for a very long period of political tumult and political contestation in Egypt. We will not come back here on February 11, 2015, and talk about a stable political order in Egypt.

Everything in Egypt now is contested and, as I said in my—in my testimony, the authorities currently only have one answer to this, and that is the use of force and coercion, which has a dynamic effect on politics.

There is something called the repression radicalization dynamic. So in a way, not to suggest that what is happening in the Sinai is a function of the July 3 coup, as I said, this is a situation that has been festering for quite some time, but the repression in the political system does create an environment where primarily angry young men may decide to take up arms to—in a way to redress their grievances because they are not able to do so through the political institutions of the state. That is a very dangerous situation.

As I said, the Egyptian government is really—it is saying that it is pursuing a political process that will lead to a democratic opening. It is hard to see how that is the case with the kinds of repressive mechanisms and policies that they are pursuing at this point.

In terms of your question, what is the capacity of the Egyptian armed forces to deal with the threat in the Sinai, it is actually limited. I think that they come to the—they come to the conclusion that they are in for a long, hard slog.

But in many ways, we have helped create a situation through our military aid program that has made it difficult for the Egyptians to fight in the Sinai. That was a strategic goal of the United States. We didn't want the Egyptians to have an ability to fight in the Sinai.

Now, 30 years on, they are confronted with a threat, a threat that we have raised with them any number of times over the course of the last decade, but they have been unwilling to prepare for it for their own reasons.

So we can offer as much advice as we have, and they seem to be taking some of it. We can reassure them of our support for them, although I think that the administration's approach to it has not exactly reassured the Egyptians on this front. We can continue to encourage the rather robust security cooperation between Egypt and Israel. We can seek to institutionalize that security cooperation.

But let's make no mistake about it. The low-level insurgency that is in the Sinai and that has reached into the Nile Valley and the connections to al-Qaeda that Mr. Joscelyn made clear is something that we are going to be living with for quite some time, and it is going to take time for the Egyptian military to be able to effectively deal with this—with this challenge. It took us many years in Iraq and Afghanistan. They are starting from a position way behind where we were in those conflicts.

Thank you.

Mr. JOSCELYN. Well, Congressman, I think you have hit on the fundamental dilemma in all of this, which is the tension between sort-of short-term counterterrorism interests and what our long-term political or democratic interests should be in any country, really.

Too often we get caught in this box between a dictator, sort-of, or a tyrannical regime and, you know, basically chaos, or—you know, or some bogeyman government. That is really the problem.

I think, basically, as we move forward here, America's role should be to encourage, however we can, to opening up the political process, which, as my colleague here said, it doesn't look like, despite the promises, that is going to happen.

You know, as you pointed out, they had millions of people in Tahrir Square and elsewhere rise up. You know, these were not al-Qaeda operatives. These were not jihadists. These were people who just wanted to escape Mubarak's regime.

Really, in this fight, what we have learned in Iraq, what we have learned in Afghanistan, what we have learned elsewhere, is that is the center of gravity against this ideology that threatens us and threatens them, the al-Qaeda ideology and the al-Qaeda organization.

To the extent the real answer is to make sure that the—we put pressure on the Egyptian government to not use too heavy of a hand to try and find the actors that they can basically work with against these entities in the Sinai, opening up the political process, but, also, you know, not using their power—the Egyptian government's power to crack down legitimate political descent under the rubric of security operations. We have seen that now with journalists and others being arrested sort-of wholesale in Egypt, and a lot of that has nothing to do with security.

So I think it is tough to do and it is easy to say that America should use its leverage to try and influence things along those lines, but that is basically what we have to do.

Mr. ELMENSHAWY. Congressman, I believe a failed state in Egypt is bad news for all Egyptians and everybody except the terrorist group; and, therefore, we have to take this issue seriously.

I believe the way forward here is to have inclusive government that will include everybody, including the Muslim Brotherhood, because they have huge base of Islamic-minded views, will be a golden opportunity for al-Qaeda to recruit them if they are not included in the political process Egypt is witnessing now. I believe we should talk to Egyptian government privately to convince them of the wisdom to be inclusive in terms of the political process way forward.

I believe, as we—as it is believed for everybody, Sinai is the hub for terrorism in Egypt. A lot of jihadists return from Iraq and from Syria, and a lot of people coming from Libya and Sudan as well, and I believe Sinai is a time bomb.

Without serious development effort inside Sinai and populating Sinai—Sinai is having only half million people in a land bigger than Jordan and Israel combined—this issue will live there. Terrorism will be a routine in Sinai without having serious development.

Cairo elites used to ignore Sinai for decades after we get back from Israel in 1970s, after the big treaty in 1979, and since then it is marginalized, ignored. No serious development there. Needs just to visit any school in northern or southern Sinai or popular coastal to know what kind of qualities they have, the locals there. I believe, without developing it and populating Sinai, there is no easy solution for the issue of radical Islam and militancy inside the Peninsula.

Mr. KING. Should have at least one more round of questions.

Again, I would ask each of you: What is the threat of foreign fighters or, if not foreign fighters, just Egyptians who are fighting in Syria now coming back to Egypt as more skilled terrorists, if you will? How much of a threat do you see that being?

Mr. COOK. Thank you, sir.

I think it is a very significant threat. Congressman Higgins raised the issue of terrorists having access to surface-to-air missiles. We know that an Egyptian helicopter was taken down by one.

I think that—and it is believed that those who perpetrated this and a number of other attacks specifically on the minister of interior and others are Egyptians who have returned from jihad in Syria.

The fact that Ayman Zawahiri, an Egyptian who is the head of al-Qaeda, has essentially extended his support to Ansar Bayt al Maqdis is an important development. Although there is a tremendous debate about where Zawahiri sits in terms of influence over al-Qaeda and al-Qaeda-affiliated groups, he is Egyptian. His entire life has been engaged in an idealogical battle against the Egyptian state.

His extension of support, his call to Egyptians to fight this illegitimate government, risks significant numbers of Egyptians who have fought in Syria and Iraq now for many years back to Sinai and poses a very significant threat.

Mr. KING. Mr. Joscelyn.

Mr. JOSCELYN. Well, the September 5, 2013, suicide bombing that targeted the Egyptian interior minister was executed by a terrorist who had fought in Afghanistan, tried to fight in Iraq, and had fought in Syria.

Just yesterday, actually, Egyptian officials said that they have been tracking the connections between his fellow plotters and what is happening in Syria, saying some of them fought with the Nusra Front, which is al-Qaeda in Syria, and that they have been tracking actually Syrians in Egypt as well.

So these threats are—we have already seen them sort of metastasized. We have already seen this happen where the threat from the dynamic play between Syria and other nations in the region, including Egypt, is well in effect.

The problem is, with the Sinai and all these things, as we have seen and, I think, principally what you are concerned about and what we have witnessed is that the threat to American interests can really manifest themselves across this network at any time. Okay?

We have seen that now with al-Qaeda in Iran, with the plot against the train going into Canada. We have seen that with Pakistani Taliban, who had a bomber placed in Times Square. We have seen that with AQAP.

The problem is that the Sinai is linked into this global network— okay?—as this Walid Badr, the suicide bomber, shows, as history shows, and the problem is that this basically means that a new threat can manifest itself through this network, through the Sinai, through Egypt, really at any time.

Mr. ELMENSHAWY. I believe, Chairman, when we talk about foreign fighters or Egyptian hold forth in Syria and places like Iraq and Afghanistan, we should talk about Egyptian borders.

Egypt border Libya and Sudan and Gaza and Israel, and I believe giving aid to Egyptian soldiers to control the border and give some training will help very much by eliminating this threat to a large extent.

Of course, intelligence hearing about these people who move freely to and from Egypt, it is very important issue. That shouldn't be neglected to fight these cross-border terrorists.

Mr. KING. One country we haven't mentioned is Jordan, which is certainly in that neighborhood, which right now is overwhelmed with refugees from Syria, surrounded by hostile countries.

Do you see any threat from any of these groups that could destabilize Jordan or any activity there just being so close in the neighborhood?

Again, Dr. Cook and Mr. Joscelyn and Mr. Elmenshawy.

Mr. COOK. Mr. Chairman, I will defer, in terms of expertise, on what is happening specifically in Jordan, but I think that it is——

Mr. KING. I was thinking more of potential threat.

Mr. COOK. Right.

I think that the huge numbers of refugees in Jordan, the pressure on that country and—combined with the very significant fight on its borders in Syria and Iraq poses a significant threat because of these—these networks.

Remember that Jordan was a target of al-Qaeda during the—our occupation—invasion and occupation of Iraq. I think that these jihadist groups see the region, broadly speaking, as one battlefield.

So I think that there is as much—the threat in Egypt is certainly far more acute because of the political situation there, but I certainly don't think that we could talk about stability in the region. I think we need to talk about relative instability.

I certainly would include Jordan and the fact that there are so many foreigners now in that country. Obviously, jihadists, as I said, see the region as one battlefield, that we have to include it as a potential—a potential problem area.

Mr. KING. Mr. Joscelyn, I guess, in addition to what Dr. Cook said, I am thinking about the ripple effect or the carry-on effect of what would happen in the Sinai affecting Jordan, even though it is not directly involved, how that could have an impact.

Mr. JOSCELYN. Well, that is certainly possible. We have already seen it the other way with Syria's ripple effects into Jordan because, in late 2012, there was actually a very complicated multi-staged attack that was planned by Nusra Front—Nusra Front fighters who were re-purposed for a terrorist attack on the U.S. embassy.

Basically, this was supposed to be a cascading attack where they were going to attack numerous targets on their way to the embassy and, as sort of security forces scrambled, then they were going to up the ante and attack our embassy. That was—that was launched by fighters who had trained and fought in Syria.

As I said a couple of times now, the point is that what is happening in Sinai is not distinct from any of these other networks. They are tied in. They are linked in. So the problem is that this can manifest itself very quickly across the network.

Mr. KING. Mr. Elmenshawy.

Mr. ELMENSHAWY. I would just add that Jordan used to have and still hundreds of thousands of refugees in Iraq and recently in Syria.

Now I look at Syria and Iraq and I believe they manage it very well so far. We don't see any Jordan-related terrorist attack in big magnitude in last few years or few months.

However, the proximity of Sinai to Jordan makes, of course, a concern, especially that militants in Egypt attack the gas line that was fought in Jordan before and Israel as well. I believe it is something we should be aware of about.

Mr. KING. My understanding is that that attack on the pipeline is—caused tremendous economic damage in Jordan.

Mr. Joscelyn, you want to say something?

Mr. JOSCELYN. Actually, that is a central feature of the propaganda that comes out of ABM and Ayman Zawahiri on the pipeline attacks. They list off a number of reasons.

One of the ABM videos I reviewed just recently has some commentator from Egypt going through all the economic damages that caused Israel and others, including Jordan.

This is a central feature in Ayman Zawahiri's talking points, that, basically, this causes great economic calamity on—you know, now, some of it is hype, but this is basically their central message.

Mr. KING. Okay. Thank you.

Mr. Higgins.

Mr. HIGGINS. Thank you, Mr. Chairman.

You know, I thought when bin Laden was captured and killed that it was going to be the end of al-Qaeda. At least some had argued that because bin Laden was the charismatic leader and, much like, you know, Nazis with Hitler, members of al-Qaeda, you know, gave a blood oath to bin Laden that, you know, he would—they would—they would follow his rule.

But it seems as though—you know, obviously, we have not had the end of al-Qaeda, but al-Qaeda-ism has seemed to have perpetrated a lot of really troubled spots, and they don't all seem to be in alignment. You know, you had that one al-Qaeda leader, Abu

Bakr al-Baghdadi in Fallujah, not entirely aligned with some of the leaders that we are traditionally familiar with.

So I suppose, you know, the one question is: In the short term, what do we fear most? Do we fear a consolidation of al-Qaeda in targeting a specific strategic area like Egypt or recruitment of new members in the short term?

Mr. JOSCELYN. Well, actually, again, I think you have hit on a fundamental question about, really, what is al-Qaeda and what it is all about.

The fundamental misunderstanding, I think, in the United States and in the West has been to always conceive of them as solely terrorists who are interested in the big mass-casualty attack.

The truth of the matter is, if you go through the strategic doctrine, if you go through what bin Laden was about, what Zawahiri is about, they have always conceived themselves as political revolutionaries. Attacking us and our interests was always a step in their long game to try and acquire political power for themselves and ideology.

Now the question becomes: How are they doing in that regard? Unfortunately in Syria, the Sinai, and elsewhere, they are doing quite well, because what is happening is they are winning new converts.

You mentioned Abu Bakr al-Baghdadi, the head of ISIS. The reason he was basically excommunicated from al-Qaeda was he didn't get that. He wasn't playing that revolutionary game very well, whereas, the guys in al-Qaeda senior leadership wanted to play that game and have designated as their appointees in Syria to play that game are playing it much better. That is the concern.

So what I say is, if you look back through the history of al-Qaeda and how mass-casualty attacks on us are manifested—okay?—including like the 9/11 plot, the pilots for the 9/11 were recruited initially to fight in Chechnya. That is what they were recruited for, an insurgency that al-Qaeda had a hand in. A couple of the musclemen for that plot actually fought in Bosnia, as Khalid Sheikh Mohammed, the mastermind of it.

So the point is that, if you look at these terrorist attacks against us, historically, they have been very much connected to these insurgencies that al-Qaeda had its footprint in.

That is really the danger, that, basically, the next Khalid Sheikh Muhammed, the next muscle hijackers, the next guys like this, could be fighting in Syria today, could be fighting in the Sinai, could be fighting somewhere else. That is what the real danger is.

Mr. COOK. If I might add, I don't disagree with anything that is said, but I think it is important, because we are talking about the Sinai, we are talking about Egypt, to recognize that in many ways Egypt is a crucible of trans-national jihadists, that the intellectual framework for the kind of terrorist threat that we are seeing now were laid in Egypt in the 1960s and 1970s.

It has come to fruition in important ways in that Egypt has produced a veritable all-star list of trans-national jihadists, and that is why Sinai and Egypt have a special place, in addition to the fact that Ayman Zawahiri is now the leader of al-Qaeda.

Certainly al-Qaeda adherents swore a blood oath to Osama bin Laden, but in many ways this is—you know, in a big way, an Egyptian organization, and that is why I think the threat from the Sinai, the support that Zawahiri has given to Ansar Bayt al Maqdis, in particular, suggests that we are going to be observing a very significant fight there for quite some time.

Mr. KING. Okay. The gentleman yields back.

Ms. Jackson Lee is here. I would just—if she has questions, we have to adjourn a hard time of 4:15. So if you——

Ms. JACKSON LEE. Thank you, Mr. Chairman.

I didn't know if the Ranking Member had posed questions already. Thank you both very much for the opportunity.

Let me just, having not sat in on the testimony—and I thank the gentlemen very much for your presence here today.

Let me go with Dr. Elmenshawy. Do I have it almost correct, Professor?

Just in light of what I am gleaning from the growing presence of al-Qaeda—I would hesitate to say epicenter—what impact will the potential elections and the potential candidacy of the head of the military, which I understand may still be a potential viable candidate, have?

Second: What is the impact of the trial of the former President Morsi with respect to the Muslim Brotherhood and its connection to al-Qaeda?

Is there—we have always looked to the agreement that we have had with Egypt and Israel for a very long time and the then-stability, at least as it relates to the relationship and the stability in the Mideast, and it does not reflect on how the Egyptians were being treated.

But what—how unstable is that area, particularly as we are looking at the negotiations between Israel and the Palestinians?

Mr. ELMENSHAWY. Thank you, Madam Congresswoman, for your question.

As for first point which Field Marshal El-Sisi expected declaration of running candidacy—his candidacy run for the president, I believe it won't affect Egypt's effort to fight terrorism at any level. I believe it is beyond the president of—the next president of Egypt.

But if the military-declared roadmap is taking place without including all political forces, it will be short of the expectation of most Egyptians and it makes—the mission and the goal of al-Qaeda is much easier to recruit angry and frustrated Brotherhood views who expected democracy to provide some opening, some place to express their wish, their desire and expectations, and now they will be banned from the political game in Egypt, which I am afraid it will let them find another way, which will be to join the militant groups in Egypt and Sinai.

So I believe the name of the next president is irrelevant to our discussion and to the threat Egypt is facing in term of growing terrorism.

As I tried for the former President Morsi, I believe it is another good tool to convince these angry Egyptians or people who believed in Morsi and voted for him, democracy doesn't work.

I believe one serious issue, he is facing serious crime, espionage, and the only punishment in Egyptian law is capital punishment.

So assuming the elected president not only in Egypt, in the entire Arab world, for the case will never have elected head of state to stand such a trial and be executed, that is what kind of message would send for young Arabs and young Egyptians?

I believe it would be a wrong message. So I hope insurgents in Cairo will be more wise to deal using political solution for this crisis, not military solution or security solution, as they do so far.

As for the Israeli, as I mention here, I believe it—the biggest group we have in Egypt now is—militant group using al-Qaeda-style attacks is Ansar Bayt al Maqdis. Its name given tell us the relation with Israel and Arab-Israeli conflict. "Ansar Bayt al Maqdis" means "companion of Jerusalem."

So Jerusalem is still in the minds and the recruiting tool for this jihadist. As long as Arab-Israeli and Palestinian-Israeli conflict is not resolved totally and fairly, I believe it will be a good opportunity to recruit more radicals and more young angry Arab and Palestinians to join the fight for al-Qaeda.

Ms. JACKSON LEE. Mr. Joscelyn, if I could quickly, then, as you listen and, I guess, as you are articulating here today, whether—whoever might be running for office in Egypt, the witness, Mr. Elmenshawy, indicated that, if you are not embracing—you still have this contingent of angry Egyptians, is that what you are speaking to in terms of the fuel for al-Qaeda and that that then can spill over into actions against the United States that we should be very wary of?

Mr. JOSCELYN. I think that is absolutely part of the problem. I think——

Mr. KING. Mr. Joscelyn, if you keep your answer to 2 minutes because we do have to adjourn at a hard time.

Mr. JOSCELYN. I will do it real quick.

Ms. JACKSON LEE. Thank you, Mr. Chairman.

Mr. JOSCELYN. I think we have already seen some poaching by ABM—that's Ansar Jerusalem—and Sinai of Muslim Brotherhood members. You can see that in some of their videos. They are capitalizing off the anger of what is going on inside Egypt.

You mentioned the trial of former President Morsi there. I think this is an important opportunity. Some of the allegations that have been made by the new Egyptian ruling regime really go far and beyond what I think are probably plausible.

They have—one of the allegations is that Morsi was actually on the phone with Ayman Zawahiri, the head of al-Qaeda, and was involved in all sorts of conspiring. This is the type of thing, I think, if you are in the U.S. Government, you should be able to challenge the Egyptian regime on and say, "Okay. Show me the transcript. Show me the audio of this alleged phone call that you are talking about."

Because it is one thing to talk about legitimate sort-of problems and legitimate security concerns. It is another to use those as tools to sort of squash political dissent.

Mr. KING. Let me——

Ms. JACKSON LEE. Thank you, Mr. Chairman. I yield back.

Mr. KING. Ms. Lee yields back. Thank you.

I want to thank the witnesses for your testimony today. Again, I apologize for the delay at the start. It was—just turned out to be one of those days, and I certainly regret that because I know the staff put a lot of work into this and the Ranking Member and I.

But you certainly—again, the testimony you provided is going to be in the record. I certainly found it very, very enlightening, very sobering, also. So I want to thank you for that and for the time you have given us.

Members of the subcommittee may have some additional questions. So if they submit them to you in writing, we would greatly appreciate you responding to them.

Ranking Member, have——

Mr. HIGGINS. That's all.

Mr. KING. Okay. Without objection, this subcommittee stands adjourned. Thank you again.

[Whereupon, at 4:15 p.m., the subcommittee was adjourned.]

○